The Role *of the* Congolese Catholic Church

The Role *of the* Congolese Catholic Church

Promotion of Economic and Social Justice in Relation to Oil

HERMANN-HABIB KIBANGOU

Foreword by Paulin Poucouta

WIPF & STOCK · Eugene, Oregon

THE ROLE OF THE CONGOLESE CATHOLIC CHURCH
Promotion of Economic and Social Justice in Relation to Oil

Copyright © 2024 Hermann-Habib Kibangou. All rights reserved. Except for brief quotations in critical publications or reviews, no part of this book may be reproduced in any manner without prior written permission from the publisher. Write: Permissions, Wipf and Stock Publishers, 199 W. 8th Ave., Suite 3, Eugene, OR 97401.

Wipf & Stock
An Imprint of Wipf and Stock Publishers
199 W. 8th Ave., Suite 3
Eugene, OR 97401

www.wipfandstock.com

PAPERBACK ISBN: 978-1-6667-7830-4
HARDCOVER ISBN: 978-1-6667-7831-1
EBOOK ISBN: 978-1-6667-7832-8

11/25/24

To Benjamin Mamvila (Coco Priso) and Maurice Kambou, both victims of the 1997 civil war in Congo and to all the victims of the civil wars in Congo.

To Nathalie Nkengue, a childhood friend who fled Brazzaville for Pointe-Noire due to the 1997 civil war; she died in 2000 in Pointe-Noire.

And to all those displaced by the civil wars in Congo.

Contents

Acknowledgments | ix

From the same author | xi

Abbreviations | xiii

Foreword: This People Is Precious in God's Sight | xv

General Introduction: The Role of the Catholic Church in Congo | xix

One: The Republic of the Congo (or Congo-Brazzaville): A Brief Description | 1

Two: The Catholic Church in Congo-Brazzaville: Its Possible Role | 11

Three: African Ethics and Management of the Common Good in Promoting Social and Economic Justice in Relation to Oil | 45

Four: Strategy of Action | 67

Conclusion: Promotion of Social and Economic Justice in the Matter of Oil | 103

Bibliography | 107

Index | 117

Acknowledgments

MY THANKS TO THE former Weston Jesuit Community in Cambridge and the New Faber Jesuit Community in Brighton for the companionship, friendship, and all kinds of support during my studies at Boston College (USA).

I am grateful to William Russel, SJ, Thomas Massaro, SJ, and Richard Lennan for helpful correction and instructive comments. Many people helped me, directly or indirectly, in the preparation of this academic work such as Lidvine Nguemeta, Stella Ifenuk, and Roger Bertrand Mouanga.

My deepest debt of gratitude to David Hollenbach, SJ, for sustaining me and helping to improve this study. My deepest gratitude also to Professor Poucouta for agreeing to write the foreword to this book.

From the same author

Social Stakes of Privatizations in Cameroon: Case of the Cameroon Development Corporation (CDC), Resource Publications, Eugene, OR, 2018, 149 p.

Enjeux sociaux des privatisations au Cameroun: le cas de la 'Cameroon Development Corporation' (CDC), Paris, Edilivre, 2009, 157 p.

La vision mvengienne de la paupérisation anthropologique. Une piste de réflexion philosophique sur le ntù? Paris, Edilivre, 2011, 112 p.

The Role of the Congolese Catholic Church in Promoting Social and Economic Justice in Relation to Oil, OutskirtsPress, Denver, CO, 2011, 133 p.

Paulin Poucouta, Le service de la parole de Dieu. Entretiens, Editions Paulines, Abidjan, 2016, 168 p.

The Mvengian Vision of Anthropological Pauperization: A Path for Philosophical Reflection on Ntù?, Wipf & Stock, Eugene, OR, 2022, 74 p.

Abbreviations

ACERAC	Association of Episcopal Conferences of the Central African Region
CEC	Episcopal Conference of Congo
CST	Catholic Social Teaching
CIDSE	International Cooperation for Development and Solidarity
SNPC	National Petroleum Company of Congo
PWYP	Publish What You Pay

Foreword

This People Is Precious in God's Sight

LET ME BEGIN BY thanking Father Hermann-Habib Kibangou, who once again shares with us his prophetic empathy for the misery of a people "sitting on oil barrels," and his passion for distributive justice for all the sons and daughters of Congo-Brazzaville.

Yes, the biblical prophet is one who is totally traversed by the spirituality and ethics of empathy. Biblical anthropology uses the image of the womb (*bétèn*) to express God's concern for his people. The image refers to a tender mother whose life-giving womb is moved with compassion by Israel's plight.[1] Divine empathy also resembles the loving heart of a father[2] or a caring brother.[3] In the face of captivity, misery, and injustice, God's empathy manifests itself in liberating gestures of justice:

I have seen the misery of my people. . .[4]

Divine empathy is also evident in Judah's debacle. Ezekiel offers us the most daring image in his book. The priest shows us God deserting the temple in Jerusalem, the Holy of Holies, to join his people in Babylon, in a pagan land.[5] God is not a prisoner of the

---

1. 1 Kgs 3:26.
2. Jer 31:20.
3. Gen 43:30.
4. Exod 3:7.
5. Ezek 11.

sanctuary. He is linked to Judah, to its history, and above all to its distress.

As a witness to divine empathy, the biblical prophet is in solidarity with his people, whose plight he shares. This is how the prophets Ezekiel and Jeremiah experienced exile, one in Babylonia, the other in Egypt. Ezekiel experienced this empathy in his own flesh. Having lost his wife, he is asked not to publicly express his grief. His grief becomes the paradigm of the exiles' misery, which is so overwhelming that they don't even have the strength to weep.

For the evangelist Matthew, Jesus' miracles bear witness to God's mercy, the mercy that lifts up the prostrate. They are signs of his pastoral empathy for men and women of all times:

Jesus went through all the towns and villages, teaching in their synagogues, proclaiming the Good News of the kingdom and healing every disease and every sickness. When he saw the crowds, he felt pity for them (word for word: "his bowels were stirred"), for they were weary and prostrate, like sheep without a shepherd.[6]

However, it is not enough to hear and echo the cry of the victims of injustice and misery. We need to dismantle its causes and mechanisms. Habib Kibangou, keen on socio-economic sciences, has taken the time and trouble to do just that. Wasn't it this exercise in critical appraisal that gave strength to the Congo bishops' document on oil? Is it not this capacity for analysis, combined with solid training, that makes the lay people of Congo Kinshasa and their various Justice and Peace commissions so effective?

But it takes commitment to get things moving. In Luke, we often find the Greek expression *ti poiôsomen*? It can be translated in three different ways. Either: "How are we going to do it?" In other words, we say resignedly that there's nothing we can do. The second translation is deliberative: "What can we do?" Or "can we do something?" Here, we hesitate. The third translation is "what should we do?" Here we find Luke's frequent call to get involved, concretely, personally, and communally.

It is in this dynamic that the spirituality of empathy and commitment was highlighted by the Second African Synod on

---

6. Matt 9:35–36.

Foreword

"Reconciliation, Justice and Peace." The situation of endemic violence and injustice in our countries demands not just compassion and fine analysis, but commitment, in the binding and military sense of the Latin term *munus*.[7] Moreover, Christians themselves are affected by injustice and misery, either as victims, predators, or accomplices, alas! To avoid falling into demagoguery and populism, the Church must live out its prophetic vocation as watchdog and awakener, through its deep empathy with the life of the people, through its witness in the efficient and transparent way it organizes itself. For a truly prophetic commitment, the Church must invest in the formation of Christian communities, as the Scheut Fathers did in the Democratic Republic of Congo, through the example of the Epiphany edition. Let's remember Pope Paul VI's famous words to the Council of the Laity in 1974: "Today's men need witnesses more than they need masters. And when they follow masters, it's because their masters have become witnesses."

By encouraging political leaders and Christian communities to invest in the humanization of the exploitation and management of oil revenues, the bishops of the Congo joined the prophetic witness of Jesus and committed themselves to living it out:

> Jesus died to bear witness to the seriousness with which we must respect others and liberate the weak. Jesus' cross is prophecy. The Word of God never leaves us at rest. It is light, strength, an incentive to go ever further in defending the dignity of this man, this woman, this child ... this humanity that is precious in God's eyes.[8]

Pr Paulin Poucouta

---

7. Benedict XVI, *Africae Munus*, 1.
8. Ps 8:4. See Évêques du Congo, "Déclaration des évêques sur le pétrole," 6.

General Introduction
The Role of the Catholic Church in Congo

IT IS NOT EASY to address the issue of the Church and that of all-out development of Africa when we know the circumstances surrounding the establishment of Christianity on the African soil.[1] In what follows, I will be raising the issue of the role of the Catholic Church in promoting social and economic justice in relation to oil. Indeed, it should be noted that the Catholic Church in Congo is becoming more and more present in pivotal areas such as human rights, democracy, justice and peace, the social and intellectual apostolate, partnership, management of natural resources (common good), etc. It is mainly on the management of oil that this study will be sketching the outlines shaping the attitude of the Catholic Church in Congo for greater transparency.

> The Congo's natural resources have always been the object of a power struggle rather than the basis for development and improvement of living conditions for its people.[2]

---

1. Eboussi-Boulaga, *A contretemps*, 11–40; Kibangou, *Mvengian Vision of Anthropological Pauperization*, 29–37.

2. Sundberg, "Class and Ethnicity," 1–15; Copinschi, "Governance in African-oil producing countries," 123–39; Favennec and Copinschi, "Nouveaux enjeux pétroliers en Afrique," 127–36.

GENERAL INTRODUCTION

In such a situation, "churches and civil society question the paradox of oil and poverty."[3] But one might ask why so much emphasis on oil.

Several reasons justify the importance. First, as a mineral, oil is a raw material of strategic importance in the world. For example, 40 percent of the world's energy needs are supplied by oil.[4] Second, oil is also a useful source of fuel for aeronautics and the automobile. Third, the absence of oil would trouble the world economy.[5] Fourth, the selling price of oil is often much greater than its cost of extraction.[6] All these reasons show the importance of oil. However, even though oil as natural resource is a gift from nature, it has been shown that "countries which are amply endowed with natural resources often grow slower than others."[7] On this point, the Congo is no exception. Like many countries, the Congo is victim of the Dutch Disease.[8]

Unfortunately, in Congo, oil is synonymous with poverty, war, corruption, embezzlement, etc.

Let us illustrate this by quoting Geraldine McDonald, who wrote these words on the Congo-Brazzaville experience:

> Some concrete experiences are useful to explore the witness of communities living out the principles and challenges of CST (Catholic Social Teaching). Congo-Brazzaville is the 3rd largest oil producer in sub-Saharan Africa. But instead of bringing prosperity, the oil boom has been accompanied by years of violent conflict and war, often fought over oil rents, 70% of the population

---

3. Secours Catholique, *Pour qui coule l'or noir?*, 3.

4. Secours Catholique, *Pour qui coule l'or noir?*, 4.

5. Secours Catholique, *Pour qui coule l'or noir?*, 4.

6. Secours Catholique, *Pour qui coule l'or noir?*, 4–6; Rickne, "Oil Prices and Real Exchange Rate," 1–26; Goldwyn, "Africa's Petroleum Industry," 2–5.

7. Rickne, "Oil Prices and Real Exchange Rate," 2.

8. Deindustrialization process. Curiously, this curse only concerns African countries south of the Sahara. While this view is shared by some authors, others believe that "there is no natural resource curse per se, but rather a scourge of bad governance revived by the combined effect of endogenous and exogenous factors" (Moumouni et al., "Vers une gouvernance globale," 374).

lives below the poverty line. In response to this situation the Catholic Justice and Peace Commission from Pointe-Noire, the oil capital on the coast, began an advocacy campaign on oil revenue management. The bishops took up their demands and in June 2002 issued a statement calling on President Sassou-Nguesso and his new parliament to pass a new oil revenue management law that would determine how revenue would be spent, and to establish a committee to monitor the fair management of oil revenues. The bishops appealed for solidarity from sister churches in Europe and the US, and in response the French Caritas, Secours Catholique, along with CRS (Catholic Relief Services) arranged an awareness-raising trip to France which, amongst other things, gave the delegation the opportunity to meet with directors of TotalFinaElf, the largest oil multinational operating in Congo-Brazzaville.[9]

These words about Congo-Brazzaville summarize very well the situation of this small oil producing country located in the Gulf of Guinea.[10] This is also confirmed by Geraldine McDonald and Ian Gary when they state that "oil fuels conflict and poverty."[11] Indeed, oil is at the root of many issues.

Oil and politics: in the sociopolitical history of the Congo, oil rhymes with politics. Indeed, "oil revenue management shows that it has played a key role in the politics"[12] of Congo. The Congolese oil is mainly exploited by French, American, and Italian firms.[13] There is a fuzzy relationship between the Congolese state and

9. McDonald, *Transparency*, 11. See also Smith, "Oil Wealth and Regime Survival," 232–46.

10. For more information see Pedde, "Myth of African Oil and Gas," 57–60. In this paper the author states that "denying the relevance of African oil and gas is certainly a mistake. But African energy potential has been often manipulated in order to be used more as a political and economic weapon" ("Myth of African Oil and Gas," 57). See also Klare and Volman, "Africa's Oil and American National Security," 226–31.

11. McDonald and Gary, "Integrated Approaches," 87.

12. ACERAC, *Church and Poverty in Central Africa: Case of Oil*, 2.

13. China is trying to find its way. For more information see Hurst, "China's Oil Rush in Africa," 1–12; Brooks, "Into Africa," 1–5.

GENERAL INTRODUCTION

those firms. Such a fuzzy relationship is manifested in the secret agreements that bind the Congolese state and the oil companies. As the bishops put it:

> There is absolute secrecy in the elaboration and signing of contracts. Revenue drawn from oil exploitation strengthens state authority, which is used to the detriment of the population. Enriched by oil dividends, the political power holders consider themselves independent of the people, to whom they no longer feel obliged to render accounts.[14]

This interpretation of the Congolese case shows that Congolese politicians have laid hands on oil, and do not render an account of the management of oil to the Congolese people. They do what they want, and nothing disturbs them because in Congo, the judiciary power depends to a great extent on the political power. In other words, the judiciary power is not free and impartial. Moreover, in the single-party system, oil as well as timber "has served as a strategic economic argument in order to maintain the regimes that give preference to personal interest to the detriment of the common good."[15]

Oil and war in Congo: The experience of Congo-Brazzaville is that "the control of oil revenues has been at the center of conflict."[16] In the 1990s, the Republic of Congo experienced three civil wars (1993–94, 1997, 1998–99). The main cause of these civil wars was the struggle among political leaders for the control of oil (Congo being then sub-Saharan Africa's fifth-largest oil producer).

Oil and economy: The Congo is known for its rich fauna and flora; its economy relies mainly on oil. Its industrial sector is underdeveloped, and most products come from outside. Although producing oil, the Congo sells very expensive oil to the Congolese.

---

14. ACERAC, *L'Église et la pauvreté en Afrique centrale: Cas du pétrole*, 3.
15. ACERAC, *Church and Poverty in Central Africa: Case of Oil*, 3.
16. McDonald and Gary, "Integrated Approaches," 91; ACERAC, *Church and Poverty in Central Africa: Case of Oil*, 4.

General Introduction

As the bishops put it, "our oil flows more for others and, as in the other economic sectors, we put up with international market law."[17]

Oil and the human and ecology: "The oil production means an ecological and social danger for the adjacent populations."[18] However, even though oil production goes on offshore "marine life is of course affected by activities linked to this type of exploitation."[19] For example, the activity of many fishermen is damaged by the exploitation of oil. In addition:

> Occasional oil spills in the sea naturally affect the environment. One study is in progress in the Congo, where changes have been noted in the seaside in oil zones.[20]

Oil and ethnicity:

> The ethnic tensions and party-linked violence which increasingly troubled daily life in Brazzaville through the early 1990s were fuelled in part by struggles between France and the USA for influence in the region.[21]

Indeed, what happened is that ethnicity has been politicized, unfortunately by some political leaders who believed that those civil wars were caused by different ethnic groups fighting one another.

> Brazzaville itself grew as a city of twin quartiers—Bakongo for 'southerners,' Poto-Poto for 'northerners,' flanking a Centreville (downtown) in which government and businessmen conducted their affairs.[22]

Oil, natural resources and poverty: Congo-Brazzaville is abundant in oil, potash, zinc, uranium, timber, as well as phosphate, natural gas, magnesium, hydroelectricity, iron, and gold. Despite these resources, "more than 70 percent of the population of this resource-rich country lives on less than $1 per day and half do

---

17. ACERAC, *Church and Poverty in Central Africa: Case of Oil*, 5.
18. ACERAC, *Church and Poverty in Central Africa: Case of Oil*, 5.
19. ACERAC, *Church and Poverty in Central Africa: Case of Oil*, 5.
20. ACERAC, *Church and Poverty in Central Africa: Case of Oil*, 5.
21. Eaton, "Diagnosing the Crisis," 48.
22. Eaton, "Diagnosing the Crisis," 48.

not have access to clean water"²³ even though the river Congo is the world's second greatest river in rate of flow, behind only the Amazon River.

Oil and suffering: With oil production at 283,000 barrels per day (2000 estimates), Congo-Brazzaville has become sub-Saharan Africa's third-largest oil producer as of 2005. In the Congolese imaginary, oil is the cause of the suffering of the Congolese. In 1999, the Congolese bishops made this statement:

> How can one understand that during the last three decades, the frequent discovery and start-up of oil wells, always important, has not been accompanied by any kind of visible sign of economic transformation or rectification of the social situation of our population?²⁴

Why is the Congolese population not benefiting from the oil rent or other national resources?²⁵ The answers to these questions will be given in the subsequent chapters of this study.

However, there are many ways to approach the issue of oil in Congo. One is to make a comparative study of Congo before and after independence. This option, although interesting, would take considerable time. It would necessitate interviewing people who have experienced the two epochs. Unfortunately, I have neither the time nor the means to do this.

Another way to deal with the management of oil in Congo is to look at the economic sphere. This option, although interesting, should be done by an economist from a macroeconomic perspective. Not being an economist, this option is not realistic for me.

There is, however, an option that seems plausible for the Congolese case: explaining poverty by the country's history and its politics as well as by its social structure.²⁶ The advantage of this

---

23. Ngouari, "Économie informelle et pratiques populaires," 76.
24. McDonald and Gary, "Integrated Approaches," 88.
25. World Bank, *Republic of Congo*, 1.
26. This answer is inspired by Volman's article "Oil, Arms and Violence in Africa," 5. In this article Volman thinks that "the impact of oil resources can vary widely, depending upon a country's history, politics, and social structure." This answer has the advantage of leaving us in the realm of natural resources,

GENERAL INTRODUCTION

is that it addresses various aspects which are interrelated. While history, politics, and social structure do not have the same level of influence, looking at these three aspects, politics seems to be the most influential for the main reason that it deals with the economic power and the management of natural resources.

In addition to this, I found it interesting to proceed with a social ethical analysis[27] of the Congolese case. Since the Congolese people are poor while Congo is a rich oil-producing country, it is logical to identify the issue of mismanagement of natural resources—which inevitably extends poverty due to corruption and embezzlement—as the primary problem threatening Congolese society. Why is it a problem?

It is a problem because more than 70 percent of the Congolese people live below the poverty line.[28] Logically they should not be so poor when their country is rich. Unfortunately, the oil revenues are not used to help the people rise out of poverty because oil revenues are used in indefensible ways by politicians. In other words, if "poverty in the Congo, in both absolute and relative terms, is widespread,"[29] it means that mismanagement of natural wealth as well as embezzlement are serious problems which aggravate poverty in the Congo.[30] Indeed, these two features threaten the cohesion and stability of any given society. A society suffering from corruption and embezzlement is always threatened with internal divisions, conflicts and the like. In this way, the Republic of Congo is no exception because its recent

especially oil.

27. Inspired by Nimi Wariboko.

28. Poverty has been aggravated in part by civil wars also known as the oil wars.

29. World Bank, *Transitional Support Strategy*, 3.

30. In the words of the World Bank, the Congo "has considerable oil resources . . . extensive tropical forests, a huge untapped hydro-electric potential, and fertile soils. However, control of the state was, and remains, synonymous with the economic struggle over the control oil." These words by the World Bank point to the weak aspects of the Congolese society: mismanagement and corruption. See World Bank, *Transitional Support Strategy*, 3.

GENERAL INTRODUCTION

history is marked by civil wars and tensions between the ruling and opposition parties.

Moreover, Congo's history is marked by youth exclusion,[31] misuse of ethnicity[32] region of origin,[33] etc. While oil has been a resource that has helped Congo to make money, unfortunately it has also been a resource that has brought death to the Congolese people. For example, "by the end of 1993, some 2,000 people had lost their lives."[34] Four years later, "more than 10,000 [were] killed when Brazzaville was razed and emptied in the war in 1997."[35] They were victims of the struggle for the control of oil by political leaders.

From this perspective it can be inferred that there are features that cause tensions, conflicts, even "fueled civil war"[36] in the Congolese society, such as mismanagement of natural resources, poverty, corruption, embezzlement, lack of justice, lack of compassion, violation of human rights, and egoism on the part of Congolese political leaders and their family members.

What role may be played by the Catholic Church in a country where more than 42 percent of the population is Catholic and where Catholics have played an important role in the public realm? I will answer this question in more detail.

In this study, "role" is to be understood as what the Catholic Church says, thinks, and does to improve the quality and sustain the economy of the Congo and its functioning. I will use the word *oil* in its general meaning, namely, the crude oil as it can be found in the liquid state in the deposits.[37] The word *barrel* is to be

---

31. Most of the political leaders do not want to hand over power to younger people.

32. Zartman and Vogeli, "Prevention Gained and Prevention Lost," 265–92.

33. World Bank, *Transitional Support Strategy*, 3; Gary and Karl, *Bottom of the Barrel*, 12–41.

34. De Beer and Cornwell, "Congo-Brazzaville," 1–7.

35. Eaton, "Diagnosing the Crisis," 48.

36. This expression is used by the World Bank in the document quoted above.

37. Secours Catholique, *Pour qui coule l'or noir?*, 18.

General Introduction

understood as a unit of volume of crude oil equivalent to 159 liters and dates to the time when barrels were used to transport oil.[38] The word *deposit* refers to underground tanks containing petroleum or gas.[39] The word *reserve* is understood as a volume of recoverable oil or gas.[40] An *oil well* is a hole in the ground for exploration and exploitation of oil. By *production* I mean the extraction phase of oil or gas from a reservoir or a deposit.[41] Another important concept for this reflection is that of social justice based on the notion of rendering to each according to his economic productivity or according to his functions, responsibilities, etc.

This study comes within the scope of social ethics and will also address political as well as theological, philosophical, socio-anthropological, and biblical data. In this reflection, I will argue that the Congolese Catholic Church might play—at the national level—an important role based on the promotion of both social and economic justice to help Congo-Brazzaville move forward.

The aim of this study is to develop an ethical framework and relational networks to explain how the Catholic Church in Congo-Brazzaville might contribute to building a theological discourse based on a procedural method of ethical analysis that implies both the management of the common good in relation to oil and a culture of social and economic justice. In Congolese society as well as in the sub-Saharan African context, ethics is based on a triple relational network: anthropocentric, cosmic, and theocentric. In such circumstances, how can religion be a vehicle that brings about an "understanding of ethics that speaks socially, 'economically' and theologically to the developments and issues" of Congolese society?[42] This will be discussed in greater detail.

This reflection is divided into four chapters. In the first chapter I present the Republic of the Congo and offer some helpful characteristics to better understand the country, its history,

38. Secours Catholique, *Pour qui coule l'or noir?*, 18.
39. Secours Catholique, *Pour qui coule l'or noir?*, 18.
40. Secours Catholique, *Pour qui coule l'or noir?*, 18.
41. Secours Catholique, *Pour qui coule l'or noir?*, 18.
42. Wariboko, "Ethical Methodology," 1.

neighborhood, and resources, as well as its people. Concretely, this chapter provides a broad view of the country in question from the historic, political, economic, and religious perspectives. The various data given might constitute specific materials in the analysis of the situation in Congo-Brazzaville.

The second chapter, unlike the first, focuses on a single element of the Congo: the Catholic Church. This chapter attempts to describe the public role of the church in the Congolese society, its duties, and the challenges it faces. The civil society has frequently demonstrated its confidence in the Catholic Church at different moments of Congolese history. Why? This chapter will try to answer this question.

The third chapter is about the management of the common good and the promotion of social and economic justice. As stated above, Congo-Brazzaville is abundant in oil, potash, zinc, uranium, wood, as well as phosphate, natural gas, magnesium, hydroelectricity, iron, and gold. Unfortunately, the Congolese population does not profit from all these resources. In such a context, what needs to be done to help the Congolese to benefit from the oil rent? Does the Catholic Church have resources, both intellectual and practical, that can influence the political leaders?

Finally, chapter 4 deals with a strategy that needs to be adopted and enacted by the Catholic Church to be an influential actor whose role is to promote "greater inclusiveness, greater justice, and higher levels of human flourishing that spur on men and women to transformative praxis."[43]

First, one must know that the construct of strategy comes from the Greek words *agein*, which means "drive," or in a figurative sense "manage"; and from *stratos*, which means "army." By extension, a strategy is a conjunction of gaits with a view to an outcome. Such an outcome could obviously be the attainment of social and economic justice for the Congolese people. On the other hand, the concept of action must be understood in its collective meaning as a movement uniting groups or individuals in a common goal of defending their interests, or in defense of an ideal. Take for example

43. Wariboko, "Ethical Methodology," 16.

the Association of the Congolese taxi drivers who advocated for better conditions of transportation and cheaper gasoline prices. Some Congolese people would benefit from this association without belonging to it. It is one example of many men and women of good will working for better living conditions in the Congolese society. However, they are not the main agents.

Secondly, there are no strategies without agents. In the Congolese situation, the Catholic Church, the Peace and Justice Commission, including churches from other countries, even men and women of good will who do their best to overcome corruption and injustice, are the agents somehow active in promoting social and economic justice.

Thirdly, in any social analysis, it is relevant to draw strategies whose aim is to improve situations where the social fabric of the society is in danger as it is in the Congolese society.

Considering this, what needs to be done is first to identify the problem and then find solutions by a profound examination—a prerequisite for the realization of a real "human flourishing (eudaimonia in the Aristotelian sense)"[44] in the Congolese society. Like most peoples of the world, the Congolese want to live happily; they want the good for their society.

Even if the good of the community coincides with that of the individual, it is clearly a greater and more perfect thing to achieve and preserve that of a community; for while it is desirable to attain what is good in the case of an individual, to do so in the case of a people or a state is something finer and more sublime.

Therefore, following the logic of this chapter, it can be inferred that nothing is crucial that doesn't deal with the happiness of the greatest number of the Congolese people. As Ignatius Loyola would say, what is for the greater number is of greater importance.

The problem of mismanagement caused, among other things, by corruption and embezzlement, has moved the Congolese society away from being a unified and united country. That is why the Catholic Church among other agents is working hard to correct such mismanagement. In her advocacy for a better use of the

---

44. Wariboko, "Ethical Methodology," 16.

natural resources, including oil, the Catholic Church is trying to promote a better Congolese society. This plea is the result of a critique and an investigation into the poverty in which most of the Congolese people live—a poverty which is a social problem that strikes the moral fabric of this small country located in the region of Central Africa, and therefore in the Congo Basin. In this chapter, I will also suggest some solutions for promoting social and economic justice for Congo.

ONE

The Republic of Congo (or Congo-Brazzaville)
A Brief Description

THIS CHAPTER GIVES A brief description of the Republic of Congo, located in Central Africa.[1] In what follows, historical, political, economic, and religious data help us to better understand this country, which at one point in its history was Africa's third-largest oil producer.

The Republic of Congo is a small country located in Central Africa; its borders touch the Democratic Republic of the Congo, the Central African Republic, Cameroon, Gabon, and Angola. With 342,000 square kilometers (132,047 square miles, about the size of California, according to Keith Klein[2]), Congo-Brazzaville's population, estimated in 2021[3] as being 5.67 million,[4] is made up of fourteen main tribes and sixty sub-tribes or ethnic groups spread

---

1. The concepts of Republic of Congo, Congo-Brazzaville as well as Congo are used interchangeably. For more information see Obenga, *Histoire sanglante du Congo-Brazzaville*.

2. Klein, *Elections in Congo*, 3.

3. In 2005, this population was estimated at four million.

4. For more information, see Banque Mondiale, "République du Congo."

over the fifteen departments that comprise the country. However, a more recent study puts the Congolese population at 6,142,180.⁵

The aim of this chapter is to provide a general overview of this small but rich country,⁶ where half the population lives in the main cities: Brazzaville (the political capital) and Pointe-Noire (the economic capital). Concretely, I offer only a general picture of the Republic of Congo. To understand the country as well as its sociopolitical story, I will offer some helpful insights or characteristics in the following categories: (1) historical data, (2) political data, (3) economic, and (4) religious data regarding this country that, like many African countries, commemorated in 2023 the sixty-third anniversary of its independence.

Historical Data

The Republic of Congo was created on November 28, 1958. From 1958 through 1960, it was "an autonomous entity within the French community"⁷ and was led by the Prime Minister Fulbert Youlou, a Catholic priest. On August 15, 1960, Congo was declared independent.

Nowadays, many people confuse the Republic of Congo and the Democratic Republic of the Congo. Such confusion obviously stems from the shared name Congo, which also refers to one of the world's greatest rivers behind only the Amazon: the River Congo.

Historically, the name Congo came from an African kingdom, the kingdom Kongo⁸ that encompassed the two contemporary Congos and Angola. In other words, both countries (the Republic of Congo and the Democratic Republic of the Congo, formerly Zaïre) "have been separate countries ever since the Democratic Republic of Congo was colonized by the Belgians, whereas

---

5. Institut National de la Statistique, *Résultats préliminaires*, ix.

6. Wykes, *Avenirs énergétiques*, 16–18. See also Fonds Monétaire International, *Études économiques et financières*.

7. Klein, *Elections in Congo*, 3.

8. Sundberg, "Christianity in Dialogue," 329–30.

The Republic of Congo (or Congo-Brazzaville)

the Republic of Congo (Congo-Brazzaville) was colonized by the French."[9]

There was at the beginning great interest on the part of various explorers who coveted Congo as one of their colonies, with the appearance of an ardent race to colonize it. Congo would have been a British colony if British authorities were not short of money. In fact, as Cassie Knight puts it,

> Britain had a chance to take control of the Congo basin in 1875 when Verney Cameron, a companion of the British explorer David Livingston, became the first European to cross Central Africa from east to west. He emerged on the Atlantic coast with a treaty signed by the chief of Katanga and said that Central Africa was a region of untapped wealth just waiting to be exploited. If ratified, his treaty would have made Congo British, but the British were not interested: their budget was already overspent, and they had too many problems on their hands in other parts of the continent.[10]

If the Republic of Congo, whose capital city is Brazzaville, is also called Congo-Brazzaville it is because of the French explorer Pierre Savorgnan de Brazza (1852–1905). Born in Brazil of Italian parents, Pierre Savorgnan de Brazza "became a French citizen in 1874." In 1880, De Brazza signed a treaty of protection with the local leader, King Iloy (also known as King Makoko). This treaty considered Mbe (the previous name of Brazzaville) as part of the French Empire. The city of Brazzaville was named after De Brazza. As the city of the Empire of French Equatorial Africa—"three times the size of France and encompassing Gabon, French Congo, Chad and the Central African Republic"[11]—Brazzaville (as capital of French Equatorial Africa) was ruled by Felix Eboué, a French governor (a native of Cayenne, in French Guyana).

---

9. Knight, *Brazzaville Charms*, 7.
10. Knight, *Brazzaville Charms*, 11.
11. Knight, *Brazzaville Charms*, 40.

The Role of the Congolese Catholic Church

Political Data

At the time of independence, Fulbert Youlou became the first Congolese president and led the country from 1960 through 1963. In 1963, Youlou decided to propose a one-party state. As a result, popular demonstrations protested such a decision and demanded that Youlou resign. Abandoned, he finally decided to resign.

After Youlou's resignation, Congo was led by a provisional government headed by Alphonse Massamba-Débat (1963–68), whose policy was based on "Bantu Socialism." Such socialism was both Christian and African, and the concept of village was understood as the living communal cell in most of the societies where the socialization of the means of production was possible. Moreover, "Bantu Socialism" rejected the struggle of classes.[12]

Nine years after its independence, Congo's political life changed with the installation of a one-party system based on "scientific socialism" led by President Marien Ngouabi (1968–77), a soldier who came to power by a coup d'état. Unlike "Bantu Socialism," "scientific socialism" was understood as a universal socialism, adaptable intelligently and consciously in each country; in other words, it was the application of Marxism as a science.[13] "In 1970 the country changed its name to the People's Republic of the Congo."[14]

In 1977, because of a coup d'état, President Ngouabi was assassinated. The same year, another soldier, Joachim Yhombi Opango, took power and led the country until 1979, before being forced to resign. In 1979, Denis Sassou-Nguesso, also a soldier, took power by means of a coup d'état; he led the country until 1991.

This survey gives an image of Congo-Brazzaville as a country of permanent political violence, where politicians fight for their own interests while Congolese people suffer. In the words of Amphas Mbow, "Congolese politics have been a cocktail of Marxist-Leninist ideological utterances, public pressure and deeply rooted

---

12. Bazenguissa-Ganga, *Voies du politique au Congo*, 98.
13. Bazenguissa-Ganga, *Voies du politique au Congo*, 98.
14. Klein, *Elections in Congo*, 3.

The Republic of Congo (or Congo-Brazzaville)

ethnic, regional and personal antagonisms."[15] The Congolese socialist regime lasted several decades until the end of the 1980s, when the Marxist-Leninist regime had reached its limits.

The management of the country became catastrophic. Workers, intellectuals, as well as churches, agreed that a political change was necessary. In the words of Abel Kouvouama, "The desire to break away from the former system had informed the role played by intellectuals, syndicates, the army, Youth and Women's Movements, as well as churches and religious sects."[16]

From a political perspective, it can be claimed that 1989 was an unforgettable year in world affairs because of the changes in Eastern Europe, whose consequences affected many African countries including Congo-Brazzaville. As a result, in 1990, the then French President François Mitterrand organized a summit in La Baule[17] (France) to encourage France's former colonies to move forward to democracy.

The same year, in September 1990, the Congolese Trade Union (CSC) led a general strike that played an important role in the advent of democracy in Congo-Brazzaville. The ruling Congolese Party (PCT, Parti Congolais du Travail) finally allowed the creation of other political parties and the organization of a National Conference from February 25 to June 10, 1991.[18] Led by a Catholic bishop, Ernest Kombo, SJ, this National Conference "took place at the convention center of Brazzaville, with 1100 delegates representing political parties, workers' unions, civil organizations . . . as well as the various denominations representatives of the state, and political and administrative personalities."[19]

In 1992, the Congo experienced its first democratic elections. A new president, Pascal Lissouba, was elected for five years. Unfortunately, from 1997 a series of three civil wars put Brazzaville

15. Mbow, *Political Transformations of the Congo*, 94.
16. Kouvouama, "Truth in Politics," 186.
17. Known as "*Sommet de la Baule.*"
18. Kouvouama, "Conférence nationale et modernité religieuse," 387–412; Kouvibidila, *Histoire du multipartisme au Congo-Brazzaville: Débuts*, 177–205.
19. Kouvouama, "Truth in Politics," 186.

on the list of the most unstable cities in the world. The main reason for these civil wars was the struggle among political leaders for the control of oil (Congo being sub-Saharan Africa's fifth-largest oil producer). After many months of violent struggle, the former president Denis Sassou Nguesso, helped by Angola, Chad, and other mercenaries, "returned (by force) in 1997 and remains Congo's president today."[20]

Economic Data

The Congolese economy is mainly based on oil. If political independence from France was quite "evident," it seems that, economically, France is still present in Congo through one of her most important corporations: former Elf Aquitaine,[21] "re-baptized Total in 2003."[22] Before 1972, oil was not a priority for the Congolese government, regarding its general revenues. Indeed, wood was then the main economic resource. This change is explained by the beginning in January 1972, of the oil exploitation, in the deposit of Emerald, by the French company Elf Aquitaine. Since May 2021, this oil company has adopted another name, becoming TotalEnergies.

In the words of Gualbert-Brice Massengo,[23] two reasons explain the beginning of the petroleum activity in Congo: the energetic power of France and the will of the Congolese post-colonial state to attract direct foreign investments. Besides the French oil company, there was its Italian competitor: Agip, a subsidiary of ENI. The motive of such investments was clear: create jobs and help the Congolese state to gain access to the main international currency, the US dollars. Nowadays, Congolese oil is mainly exploited by US, French, and Italian companies.

From an economic perspective, oil is seen as the most important natural resource in Congo, as well as "the root of Congo's

20. Knight, *Brazzaville Charms*, 12–13.

21. Whose agreement of establishment was signed with the Congolese state on October 17, 1968.

22. Koula, *Pétrole et violences au Congo-Brazzaville*, 9.

23. Massengo, *L'économie pétrolière du Congo*, 66.

The Republic of Congo (or Congo-Brazzaville)

problems."[24] Besides oil, Congo has timber, diamonds, manganese, etc., exploited by different companies. However, emergent countries like China are becoming more and more present in the Congolese economy. According to Amphas Mbow, "Yet the revitalization of the Congolese economy has not yet happened. The central problem—the lack of management—reflects that."[25] One of the reasons that explains this lack of management is the fact that oil revenues have not been used in a proper way since the oil boom in 1982. The truth of the matter is that "dependence on oil had a negative impact on the economic and social structures of the country, to the point that where it had created excessive expectations of future income based on unreliable estimates of the behavior of the oil market."[26] In other words, Congo-Brazzaville committed a major error by basing its economy exclusively on oil.

Besides this fact, the economy of this country also depends on its neighbors. That's why it is impossible to understand the Congolese economy without taking into consideration its relations with other countries. In the words of Rémy Bazenguissa, the relation of the Congo and the other countries is of two types: extra-African and continental.

From the first type (extra-African), it can be inferred that despite the Congolese independence, France still interferes in Congolese politics when oil policy is involved. That is what happened in 1997, during the civil war, when the elected president Pascal Lissouba wanted a new policy based on an improvement of future oil revenues, with a new contract governing shared production, oil negotiation with different ministers, and not only with the president alone as it was done before. This new policy was not appreciated by Elf authorities, who had a different relationship with Denis Sassou-Nguesso. That is why they decided to finance his militia with mercenaries and arms to remove Lissouba from power. As a result, Sassou-Nguesso won the 1997 war with the help of soldiers

---

24. Knight, *Brazzaville Charms*, 12.
25. Mbow, *Political Transformations of the Congo*, 2.
26. Mbow, *Political Transformations of the Congo*, 85.

from Angola, Chad, and mercenaries from other countries. Not to mention the tacit support of the Chirac government.[27]

Lissouba's new policy created a conflict between France and the US, as well as between Congolese political leaders. As Daniel Volman puts it:

> Although essentially a conflict between the leaders of rival ethnic groups, the civil war also took the form of a proxy war between rival U.S. and French oil companies. The French national oil company (now TotalFinaElf) had a longstanding relationship with General Sassou-Nguesso during his years in office and funded the creation of his private army, which ultimately took control over most of the country. President Lissouba, on the other hand, had begun to open up the country's oil fields to exploitation by a U.S. oil company, Occidental Petroleum, which helped fund and equip Lissouba's troops.[28]

This conflict between a Congolese president and Elf was not the first such episode in the history of the country. According to Yitzhak Koula, Commander Marien Ngouabi was assassinated with the complicity of Elf Aquitaine. For Yitzhak Koula, "on March 13, 1977,[29] President Ngouabi denounced publicly physical threats on his person by French imperialism and its vassals."[30] Five days later, Marien Ngouabi was assassinated. Before that, he accused Elf of cheating on the extraction of Congolese oil.[31] For the president, Elf did not provide an accurate account of the number of barrels of oil exploited in Congo.

As a matter of fact, oil is one of the reasons for violence in Congo while the Congolese population does not benefit from oil revenues. This is a bitter observation in a country rich in resources

---

27. For more information, see Editions L'Harmattan, "Petrole et Violences."

28. Volman, "Oil, Arms and Violence," 3.

29. The year 1977 is an unforgettable year in Congo. Five days after the assassination of President Ngouabi, Cardinal Emile Biayenda was killed. The same year former president Alphonse Massambat-Debat was also killed, as well as many other people.

30. Koula, *Pétrole et violences au Congo-Brazzaville*, 30.

31. Koula, *Pétrole et violences au Congo-Brazzaville*, 30.

and where 70 percent of the population lives below the poverty line.

From the second type (continental), the economy of Brazzaville depends on the economy of its neighbor Kinshasa. In fact, Kinshasa supplies Brazzaville with products like meat, poultry, fish, etc. Such a relation between the two closest capital cities in the world is usually complicated by the closing of the river port whether in Kinshasa or in Brazzaville.

Religious Data

About 88 percent of the Congolese declare themselves as Christians; 2 percent are Muslims and 2.8 percent of believers come from traditional religions.[32] Other sources put forward the figure of 89.9 percent Christians, including 62 percent Catholics, 12.7 percent Protestants.[33]

If the Catholic Church is the majority church, some churches[34] like the Evangelical (the largest Protestant church), the Kimbanguist Church,[35] the Greek Orthodox Patriarchate of Alexandria, as well as the Salvation Army, and the Lutherans are also present in Congo as members of the Ecumenical Council of Congo.

Being the majority church, the Catholic Church has been playing an important role in Congo. As stated above, the first Congolese president was a Catholic priest (Fulbert Youlou). Another Catholic priest (Bishop Ernest Kombo) led the National Conference as well as the Superior Council of the Republic, the Transitional Parliament.

Another aspect is that the church tries also to be visible in the media. *La Semaine Africaine,* founded in 1952 by the Catholic

---

32. US Department of State, *Republic of Congo 2022*, 1–2.

33. Biyela, "Trajectoires de l'Église de Zéphirin," 47.

34. Dorier-Apprill and Ziavoula, "Diffusion de la culture évangélique," 129–56.

35. Whose founder is Simon-Pierre Kimbangu, from the Democratic Republic of the Congo (DRC, formerly Zaïre).

The Role of the Congolese Catholic Church

Church, is known as one of the most widely read and respected bi-weekly newspapers in the country.

The information about the Catholic Church will be helpful to understand its role and responsibility in Congolese politics as will be treated in the second chapter.

In this chapter I focused on various data about the Republic of Congo that provide an interesting overview of this country located in Central Africa, more precisely in the Congo Basin. I first presented historical data to show that Congo, being a small country, is also a country rich with natural resources like timber, zinc, gas, and manganese that constitute real (interesting) potentialities to attract investors. Unfortunately, in Congo the entire economy is based on oil.

The economic data have shown that "oil also played a central role in the civil war in the Congo Republic."[36] In other words, oil is a cause of political violence in Congo. I tried also to show that France is very involved in the Congolese economy because of oil controlled by her main corporation, formerly Elf, now Total Energies. This situation does not help the country to improve its economy if oil is controlled by non-nationals and as long as it remains the main economic resource of the country.

In a political perspective, the political data have shown that Congo is a state in "construction," divided and in need of genuine democracy to move forward. If the divisions among political leaders have been one of the causes of ethnic confrontations, Congolese people exercising prudence vis-à-vis their politicians have believed in the church. In this perspective the church in Congo appears as the most important body of the civil society; therefore, it must play an important role that can help this country to move forward.

---

36. Volman, "Oil, Arms and Violence," 3.

TWO

The Catholic Church in Congo-Brazzaville
Its Possible Role

"Ce qui a été accompli permet de mesurer ce qu'il reste à entreprendre."
FABIEN EBOUSSI-BOULAGA

THIS SECOND CHAPTER BRIEFLY presents the Catholic Church in the Congo, trying to understand its sociological role as a critic of Congolese society, while at the same time making its own self-criticism. Using a socio-historical approach, this chapter looks at several aspects of this church: evangelization of the Congo, the Episcopal Conference of the Congo and its various commissions, its relations with other churches, the function of the Church, and so on. In this context, the 2002 bishops' declaration on oil management is of paramount importance. Authors such as Rahner, Poucouta, and Ngoïe-Ngalla provide interesting insights into the Church's critical and self-critical function.

In the essay "The Congolese Church: Ecclesial Community within the Political Community," Yvon Christian Elenga, SJ,

The Role of the Congolese Catholic Church

"examines how the Roman Catholic Church has tried to enliven the ecclesial community within the Congolese political community in order to promote the creation of a more just society."[1] In the same perspective, Daniel Kasomo states: "The question therefore, is not whether the churches should be involved in politics but how and to what extent the church can contribute to democratic politics without losing sight of its mission, vision and indeed, credibility."[2]

In what follows, regarding the Congolese Catholic Church, I focus on an "appropriate relation between religion and politics,"[3] but with an additional emphasis on a mutual solidarity between them, in both the domestic realm as well as the international realm.[4] This additional emphasis deals with the relationship existing within the Congolese Catholic Church and between the Congolese Church and other churches or organizations.

This chapter also explores several aspects of the role the Congolese Catholic Church has to play internally in Congo, conscious of its influence within Congolese political and social life. Concretely, it addresses the issue of the Catholic Church in Congo-Brazzaville and its function within the Congolese society, a function that Karl Rahner would call "the function of church as a critic of society."[5]

In fact, following Rahner, "the function of the church as a critic of society" "has the utmost relevance to the contemporary situation." Based on the assumption that the Church "shall take part with 'people' in their struggle," such a function is one of the utmost characteristics of what is known today as "political theology," also known as "a theology of revolution and force."[6]

In this chapter, I contend that the Congolese Church is the fruit of its history as well as the fruit of the larger Roman Catholic

---

1. Elenga, "Congolese Church," 245.
2. Kasomo, "Examination of Co-Existence," 130.
3. Hollenbach, *Global Face of Public Faith*, ix.
4. Ming Wong, "Catholicity and Globality," 459–75; Miller, "Where Is the Church?," 412–32.
5. Rahner, "Function of the Church," 229–49.
6. Rahner, "Function of the Church," 229–49.

Church. In other words, one cannot understand the Congolese Church's role by ignoring either it is its history or the Roman Catholic Church's history.

With this end in view, the whole Congolese Catholic Church can be understood from either a national perspective or a continental perspective. Both perspectives provide a brief historical overview of evangelization in Africa and evangelization in Congo. Indeed, to understand the Catholic Church in Congo, a link between the two perspectives is helpful for two main reasons. Firstly, it helps one understand why "the recent wave of democratization in Africa has enabled the Roman Catholic Church to participate in the political life of several African countries, including the Republic of the Congo."[7] Secondly, it makes one understand what duties and challenges the church in Congo must face, being both a national religious actor as well as a member of a transnational religious actor: the Roman Catholic Church.[8] However, for practical reasons, and to be faithful to the theme of this reflection, I shall begin directly by treating a significant experience in the life of the Church in Congo: evangelization.

This chapter proceeds as follows. First, it focuses on the Catholic Church in Congo in terms of evangelization, framework, and instrument of critique of the Congolese society. Secondly, it provides a theological analysis of the Catholic Church in the Congo. Third, it draws some considerations based on the confidence of the Congolese people in the Catholic Church (how the Church is seen by Congolese society). Finally, it provides an overview of the possible role of the Church in the Congo.

Evangelization of Congo

To some extent, the evangelization of Congo runs parallel to the colonization of Congo. This section provides a general view of the

---

7. Elenga, "Congolese Church," 245.
8. Haynes, "Transnational Religious Actors," 143.

The Role of the Congolese Catholic Church

Roman Catholic Church in Congo, from her composition to what constitutes her unity: the Congolese Episcopal Conference.

Formerly, the Republic of Congo was evangelized by the Holy Ghost Missionaries. Among them were Bishop Carrie, Apostolic Curate of Loango, and Bishop Augouard, Apostolic Curate of Brazzaville, both French, and by many other Holy Ghost Missionaries. Whereas the Congregation of the Holy Ghost was the first to evangelize the Republic of Congo, nowadays, many congregations such as the Dominicans, the Jesuits, the Holy Ghost Missionaries, and many other Catholic orders and congregations, as well as religious institutes, are present in Congo. This is, obviously, a sign that the Congolese Church has grown.

Although my interest is not to present the entire Catholic Church, but to focus on her role in promoting social and economic justice in relation to oil, I have felt obliged to present the structure of the Roman Catholic Church in Congo.

Framework of the Congolese Catholic Church

The Congolese Catholic Church is a young church that has nevertheless played an important role in the history of the country. It is divided into nine dioceses, six dioceses and three archdioceses. Brazzaville, Pointe-Noire, and Owando are archdioceses recognized as ecclesiastical provinces. Pointe-Noire is the ecclesiastical province of southwest. The ecclesiastical province of Owando (ecclesiastical province of the north) is made up of the suffragan dioceses of Ouesso and Impfondo. The ecclesiastical province of Pointe-Noire (ecclesiastical province of the south) is made up of the suffragan dioceses of Nkayi and Dolisie. Brazzaville, the ecclesiastical province of the center, includes Kinkala and Gamboma. All these dioceses and archdioceses are growing in terms of structures as well as in terms of believers.

In sum, this overview of the Congolese dioceses highlights the framework of the Congolese Church overall. Moreover, it provides helpful insights into the Congolese Church, and helps one understand what constitutes the major instrument of the Roman

Catholic Church in Congo in terms of national policy: the Congolese Episcopal Conference.

The Congolese Episcopal Conference and Its Commissions

"La question du pétrole a fait l'objet d'une réflexion pastorale profonde de la part de l'Eglise qui est au Congo et en Afrique Centrale, eu égard à la situation de grande pauvreté qui, paradoxalement, caractérise la population habitant cet espace 'quasi maudit où coule l'or noir.'"

BISHOP LOUIS PORTELLA MBUYU

In this section, I present the Congolese Episcopal Conference and its different commissions. This is relevant for two reasons. First, it sets up the core of the reflection of the Roman Catholic Church in Congo. Second, it serves to clarify the role of the Roman Catholic Church in Congo regarding public matters. In other words, it promotes an *"appropriate relation between religion and politics."* Third, it shows the nature of the relationship between Congo-Brazzaville and her partners such as the Association of Episcopal Conferences of the Central African Region (ACERAC), *"Secours Catholique,"* Catholic Relief Services (CRS), and the Conference of the US Catholic Bishops, Medicus international (ACERAC 2008), as well as Pax Christi, Caritas Europa or CIDSE.[9]

As has been pointed out above, the Congolese Catholic Church is made up of nine dioceses. Being an important body in Congolese society, "the church has enjoyed a relatively cooperative relationship with successive regimes ruling the Congo."[10] The whys and wherefores of such a position are explained by the history of Congo, and by the dominating place she occupies in the Congolese public sphere, in both the religious realm as well as the political realm.

---

9. McDonald, *Transparency*, 1–14. See also ACERAC, *La bonne gestion dans l'Église*.

10. Elenga, "Congolese Church," 246.

The Role of the Congolese Catholic Church

The first chapter provided sufficient and useful information. Therefore, without insisting too much on the religious personalities who have influenced the Congolese political realm, the following will focus on the body which represents the Roman Catholic Church in Congo, with special attention to one of its commissions: the Episcopal Commission for social pastoral and development. Here it will be useful to determine the possible role that the Congolese Episcopal Conference can play.

The Congolese Episcopal Conference

This conference is made up of all the bishops of the Congolese Catholic Church. The Congolese Episcopal Conference is currently led by Bienvenu Manamika, archbishop of Brazzaville. Divided into many commissions, the Congolese Episcopal Conference discusses problems confronting the Church in Congo and seeks solutions to those problems.

In addition to this, the Congolese Episcopal Conference has various responsibilities. The first responsibility is to take care of the believers in spiritual matters. The second responsibility is to intervene in the public sphere when the lives of believers and non-believers are in danger. This last responsibility helps one to understand the functioning of the Church as a critical eye of Congolese society. This will be explained further, after a brief overview of the various commissions that constitute the Congolese Episcopal Conference.

The Commissions of the Congolese Episcopal Conference

This section presents the various commissions that represent the Catholic Church in Congo. However, it gives a special attention to the commission for social pastoral and development which encompasses Caritas-Congo, Justice and Peace, and CEMIR.[11]

---

11. Conférence Épiscopale du Congo, "Accueil."

Within this commission, "Justice and Peace" is by far the most important regarding the problem of oil for two reasons. Firstly, it deals with problems that threaten justice and peace in Congolese society. In other words, the main goal of this sub-commission is to promote peace and justice in Congo. Secondly, "Justice and Peace" is a member of the coalition or international campaign "*Publiez ce que vous Payez*" (translated as "Publish What You Pay").[12]

Episcopal Commissions	President
	Vice-president
Doctrine of the Faith	Bishop Ildebert Mathurin MOUANGA
	Archbishop Bienvenu MANAMIKA B.
Catechesis and Evangelization	Bishop Ildebert Mathurin MOUANGA
	Bishop Toussaint NGOMA-FOUMANET
	Secretary: Br. Jean NKOMBO BOUTSOKI
Children and Youth	Bishop Daniel MIZONZO
	Bishop Urbain NGASSONGO
	Chaplain: Fr. Clotaire Jonas BANGUI
	Secretary : Chancel LIKOUKA
Liturgy	Bishop Victor ABAGNA-MOSSA
	Secretary: Abbot Jean BADINGA
	Vice-secretary: Abbot Bertin FOUETI
Consecrated life	Secretary: Sr. Josiane MOUKOKO
	Vice-secretary: Fr. Ilitch EWOLO
Lay apostolate	Bishop Armel Gélase KEMA
	Toussaint NGOMA-FOUMANET
	Coordinator: Mr. Firmin BONZANGABATO
	Secretary: Br. Jonas KITELEMONO

12. For more information see Afeikhena et al., "Addressing Oil Related Corruption," 7–32. According to them, "The PWYP campaign already has the support of over 130 groups from all around the world. Several large natural resource extraction companies, including BP, Shell, and New Mining, have expressed positive views about it" ("Addressing Oil Related Corruption," 21).

Health and pastoral care	Bishop Toussaint NGOMA-FOUMANET
	Bishop Bienvenu MANAMIKA B.
	Member: Dr. Bienvenu OSSEBI-IBARA
Social communications	Bishop Daniel NZIKA
	Secretary: Albert MIANZOUKA
Semaine Africaine	Director: Mr. Albert MIANZOUKOUTA
Magnificat Radio	Sr. Marie Colette LABAKI
Vatican radio correspondent	Mr. Sévérin MOUSSAVOU
Saint Paul printing house	Director: Mr. Paul KIMPAKOL
	Vice-director: André FOUKA
Christian Education	Bishop Daniel NZIKA
	Secretary: Sr. Clarisse NKOURISSA
	Vice-secretary: Mr. Raoul SIKA
Clergy and Seminaries	Bishop Daniel Mizonzo
Ecumenism and inter-religious dialogue	Bishop Daniel NZIKA
Family pastoral care	Bishop Urbain NGASSONGO
	Coordinator: Sr. Rolande MILANDOU
	Secretary: Mr. Roger NIOLI
Justice and Peace	Bishop Toussaint NGOMA-FOUMANET
	Coordinator: Abbot Guy Noël OKAMBA
Caritas Congo	Bishop Toussaint NGOMA-FOUMANET
	Bishop Urbain NGASSONGO
	General secretary: Mr. Alain Robert MOUKOURI
Migrants and Refugees (CEMIR)	Bishop Armel Gélase KEMA
	General secretary: Mrs. Claudia OGNELET
Spokesperson and public relations	Bishop Urbain NGASSONGO
	Secretary: Abbot Brice Armand IBOMBO
Economic council	Bishop Toussaint NGOMA FOUMANET
	Bishop Daniel NZIKA

Charismatic renewal	Bishop Bienvenu MANAMIKA BAFOUAKOUAHOU
	Bishop Daniel NZIKA
Pontifical missionary works	Bishop Ildebert Mathurin MOUANGA
Military chaplaincy	Bishop Urbain NGASSONGO
Executives and politicians	Bishop Ildebert Mathurin MOUANGA
Catholic University	Bishop Ildebert Mathurin MOUANGA
	Bishop Armel Gélase KEMA
Legal affairs	Bishop Armel Gélase KEMA
	Bishop Bienvenu MANAMIKA B.
	Secretary: Fr. Armel BADI
	Bailiff: Mr. Simplice LIMBA
	Magistrate: Mrs. Nuptia NTALANI
	Member: Abbot Guy Noël OKAMBA
Spokesperson and public relations	Bishop Urbain NGASSONGO
	Secretary: Abbot Brice Armand IBOMBO

Source: Episcopal Conference of Congo, 2024

The Episcopal Commission for Social Pastoral and Development Pastoral Care

Regarding problems that challenge peace and justice in Congo, the sub-commission "Justice and Peace" raised questions regarding how oil is managed by political leaders. By demanding that the Congolese government publish the oil revenues, two of its members, namely Brice Makosso and Christian Mounzeo, were arrested for taking part in the campaign "Publish What You Pay." Their mistake was to insist on a policy of transparency in the management of oil by the Congolese government. No one ignores the effects of mismanagement of natural resources in Congo, including oil. This is why:

The Role of the Congolese Catholic Church

> Church and civil society groups alike have increasingly called on governments and oil companies to be more transparent in their operations and financial dealings. With information on the amount of money received by their governments, church leaders, civil society groups and ordinary citizens can use what political space exists to try to hold their governments to account.[13]

Indeed, these words from Ian Gary and Terry Lynn Karl sum up the purpose of the campaign "Publish What You Pay." Concretely, they explain the mission of the sub-commission "Justice and Peace" in Congo.

Such a mission is, without doubt, the result of a real critique; it also demands a sociological analysis to comprehend the reality of any given society, including the Congolese society. It is no exaggeration to say that this mission is especially reinforced by the relationship that the Congolese Catholic Church has with her foreign partners.

The Relationship between the Congolese Catholic Church and Other Churches or Organizations

The Catholic Church in the Republic of Congo maintains a good relationship with her partners such as *Secours Catholique*, the other Catholic Churches in the Central African region, and the U.S. Bishops Conference.[14] Such a relationship helps Congolese bishops to strengthen their action at the international level. At this level, *Secours Catholique* and the U.S. Bishops Conference have played and are still playing an important role to promote social and economic justice in Congo.

This relationship must be placed under the principle of solidarity between northern and southern churches. The principle of solidarity is summarized in three main points:

---

13. Gary and Karl, *Bottom of the Barrel*, 6.

14. See U.S. Bishops Conference, *Call to Solidarity with Africa*; Secours Catholique, *Congo Brazzaville*; Linden, "Global Church in the Twenty-First Century," 261–82; Schroeder, "What of Mission," 112–26.

- As enshrined in the principle of solidarity, churches in the north and south should stand side-by-side with sister churches in Central Africa in calling for the transparent, humane, and sustainable exploitation of natural resource wealth which prioritizes the needs of the poor.
- Churches in the north should use their institutional power to gain access to policy makers to bring the concerns of those at the grassroots in oil-producing countries to the centers of power in northern countries, where many oil and mining companies are headquartered.
- Churches should support local NGO initiatives on good management of resources and challenge their local governments on transparency.[15]

These recommendations of the churches in the south to those in the north show the strong determination of the churches in the south to promote social justice in Africa.

To sum up, the Church in Congo is playing an important role by insisting on a policy of transparency in the management of oil. To strengthen her action, she has received the support of international agents such as the *Secours Catholique* or the American Bishops.

Such action can be strengthened if the Church fully understands and embraces her function of social critique or social analysis.

The Congolese Catholic Church as a Critic of the Congolese Reality

This section discusses what might be described as the function of the Roman Catholic Church in Congo. My interest here is first to explain such a function by following Karl Rahner, who makes an interesting analysis of the Church as a critic of society. And secondly, through the bishops' letter of June 2002. Finally, we will

15. McDonald, *Transparency*, 13.

analyze the critic of Congolese society by two Congolese authors: Ngoïe-Ngalla and Poucouta.

The Church as a Critic of Society

"The Function of the Church as a Critic of Society" is an article by Karl Rahner in which the author interprets in different ways what might be the function of the church. From the outset, Rahner thinks that this subject "has the utmost relevance to the contemporary situation."

The article begins with the reason why "students" are in "revolt against the ideologies and institutions of a society that has become established and 'frozen.'" In other words, according to Rahner, the students want the Church to "take part with them in their struggle." What is underlined here is any sociological issue that "students," or people who claim themselves as Christian or not, face in their everyday lives. The phenomenon of response to sociological issues, regarding the Church, says Rahner, is not new because "several of the encyclicals of John XXIII and Paul VI are concerned with sociological issues and with a critique of society. . . . The task of the Church or of the Churches as providing a critique of society is a theme that is actual and relevant today."[16] In other words, the function of the Church as a critic of society has been encouraged by popes who thought that it was necessary for the church to engage society in this way. This is true from a social perspective as well as from the historical perspective.

From a social perspective, one cannot understand the function of the Church if he or she ignores the place of the Church in society. Similarly, the Church cannot ignore the situation of believers or non-believers in society. However, this has often been the case, at least in countries where the function of the Catholic Church was portrayed as related strictly to the care of the human soul. Indeed, a long time ago, Christians thought that the responsibility of the Church was to take care only of souls. But how can one

---

16. Rahner, "Function of the Church," 230.

take care of the soul and forget the body? Unfortunately, countries like Argentina made this mistake before realizing that the Church has also to take care of both bodies and souls. This was during the dictatorship of the military regimes (in the 1970s and the 1980s). Indeed, because of the military regime, the Argentinian Church[17] decided to engage herself both in the care of the body and in the care of the soul.

What is interesting here is the fact that the Argentinian Church was aware of her real function, namely the "function of the Church as a critic of society." As Rahner puts it, "A critique of the Church is implicitly involved in the church's understanding of her own nature."[18]

In the words of Rahner, there are three ways to understand the "function of the Church as a critic of society." The first way is the principle, namely "a critique of the church is implicitly involved in the Church's understanding of her own nature."[19] Here, the church has no choice but to understand her nature by herself. This is important for two main reasons. Firstly, the Church must realize by herself that she is Church in a given society; therefore, she cannot ignore the problems that face that society. Secondly, the Church cannot remain silent but must raise her voice about difficulties that people face in that society. It is only by doing so that the church can rise to the challenge.

The second principle is that of "the self-critical church as an authoritative critic of society." Concretely, as an authority, the church must be critical of herself. This is true for three reasons. First, one must be able to "distinguish between criticism of society on the church's part and political action."[20] For Rahner, one must avoid certain misunderstandings. "*The function of the church as a critic of society is not intended to conjure up the idea of a church actively engaged in politics.*"[21] Even though this has been present in

---

17. For more information see Thornton, *Imagining Argentina*.
18. Rahner, "Function of the Church," 230.
19. Rahner, "Function of the Church," 230.
20. Rahner, "Function of the Church," 233.
21. Rahner, "Function of the Church," 233.

The Role of the Congolese Catholic Church

the history of the Church for good or for bad, the function of the church, says Rahner, is not to undertake explicitly political action. The second reason is that of "the origins of the perspective provided by the Church as critic of society as found in the gospel."[22] Rahner thinks that "the Church herself needs to be brought back ever anew by her own Spirit to this gospel as providing the perspective for social criticism."[23] In other words, the church needs to be renewed by the Holy Spirit, by looking at the history, "to which the history of the world itself belongs."[24] Such a reason is also present in the critique of the Church made by the Congolese bishop Louis Portella Mbuyu when he reminds us that the function of the church is that of a "watchman," following the prophet Ezekiel.[25] Finally, the last reason deals with "the upholders of the function of criticizing society in the church."[26] By the word "upholders," Rahner understands the "official Church" or "hierarchy." However, if the "students" criticized the "appointed authorities," it was because of "their lack of commitment to social criticism."[27] For Rahner, the function of criticizing society by the officially appointed authorities as such "has hardly been thought out as yet at the theological level."[28] This is a real problem because "the Church's function as a critic of society can hardly be subsumed under any of these three official functions of the hierarchy,"[29] namely the official church, the hierarchy, and the officially appointed authorities. Such a problem is explained, according to Rahner, by the fact that "the function of the official authorities of the Church as critic of society has still not found any clear theological topos for itself."[30] Unless man takes responsibility by recognizing this theme as a

22. Rahner, "Function of the Church," 235.
23. Rahner, "Function of the Church," 235.
24. Rahner, "Function of the Church," 235.
25. Portella Mbuyu, "Insiste à temps," 4.
26. Rahner, "Function of the Church," 242.
27. Rahner, "Function of the Church," 242.
28. Rahner, "Function of the Church," 242.
29. Rahner, "Function of the Church," 242.
30. Rahner, "Function of the Church," 243.

social challenge as well as a fact, and therefore something that needs to be planned, the fact of criticizing society by the official church "has still not achieved any theological definition and so too any recognized position in theology."[31] In other words, Rahner points out the fact that there is no theological recognition of the function of the official church as critic of society. However, this may change if a theological definition is achieved. Then, says Rahner, it is possible to speak of a "prophetic instruction." According to him, the prophetic instruction is different from a theoretical teaching. Besides, this prophetic instruction deals with a "practical appeal to the freedom of Christians and of the world." This could be called the function of social criticism as prophetic instruction because it is a "conclusion deduced from general Christian norms,"[32] but also because it is "sustained by the spirit of Jesus."

In fact, one should be aware of the period in which these words were written, namely, 1974. Fifty years later, the situation has changed because "political theology" is almost a well-known domain in theology. That is to say, the non-recognition of any theological definition of the official church as a critic of society must be nuanced.

The function of the church as a critic of society is valid and applicable in any secular society, including the Congolese society. What is interesting in the Congolese case is the fact that we have bishops who have raised their voice and addressed the Congolese political leaders. This engagement by the Congolese bishops is not contrary to what Rahner has pointed out; therefore, it does not undermine either the social teaching of the church or the spirit of Christ. Such engagement by the Congolese bishops is important because it helps one become aware of what might be the Congolese ethos. However, it is impossible to understand the Congolese ethos without a social analysis of Congolese reality. Indeed, Congolese bishops have already conducted a critique of the Congolese society, following Rahner. The 2002 bishops' declaration is well worth remembering.

31. Rahner, "Function of the Church," 243.
32. Rahner, "Function of the Church," 244.

The Role of the Congolese Catholic Church

Brief Reminder of the Bishop's Declaration of 2002

This is a letter from the bishops of Congo, consisting of an introduction followed by eight parts: (A) What the Church asks, (B) Evangelizing mission of the Church, (C) The living tradition of the Church, (D) Socio-economic reasons, (E) Ethical reasons, (F) Appeal to the international community, (H) Appeal to ecclesial solidarity. This letter is the fruit of a meeting of Congolese bishops, gathered in special session in Brazzaville from June 4–7, 2002. It was written in a context in which the Congo produces 339,000 b/d of oil, making it the third-largest oil producer in sub-Saharan Africa.[33] Paradoxically, while on the economic front this situation is a real boon, on the social front the population is living in extreme poverty, with living conditions going from bad to worse. The declaration by the Congolese bishops will have a remarkable impact on the population, as it will enable tongues to be loosened, calling the political authorities to account for their management of black gold. Without a doubt, this letter will have an undeniable influence, with the Congolese bishops moving from questioning to commitment,[34] inviting everyone to assume collective and individual responsibility. This provoked violent reactions from the political services, who questioned the position of the bishops, asking in passing whether their role was political or not. Although the letter is addressed primarily to the latter, it also includes other addressees (Christian Catholics, economic operators, oil companies, sister churches). From my point of view, to say that the Church is playing politics by making such remarks is either an erroneous analysis or simply bad faith. The Church's role is critical from the outset. A criticism that is also self-critical. It's as if we wanted to pit faith against reason. Should we, for example, reproach the Church for building hospitals, schools, or universities where the State has none? In such a context, we'd be tempted to paraphrase Jesus and say: whoever criticizes the bishops for lying, throw a stone at them. For, as the late Bishop Albert Ndongmo so aptly put it, "The

---

33. Pigeaud, "Congolais veulent leur part," 1.
34. Évêques du Congo. "Pétrole et la mission," 1–6.

Church cannot lead men to heaven as if the earth did not exist."[35] The letter from the Congolese bishops, it should be emphasized, would inspire the ACERAC text (2002) and would also serve as a basis for the text published by the Angolan episcopate.[36] Indeed, the quintessence of such a letter cannot be understood without grasping the role of the Church as a critic of society.

From the same perspective, society, like the Church, also need to be criticized, of constructive criticism. In this sense, two Congolese authors do it so well through their writings.

The Critique of Congolese society by Ngoïe-Ngalla and Poucouta

These two authors provide an enriching analysis of Congolese society. They do it so eloquently.

Dominique Ngoïe-Ngalla's article (1994) "La démission des hommes de prière et de culture" ("The resignation of men of prayer and culture") is brilliant and provocative. Although thirty years old, this article, linked to the dark history of our country, should awaken the conscience of its sons and daughters. In it, the author affirms his disappointment, anger, and discontent inherent in the unfortunate events that plunged the country into mourning. So, he writes, "It took this upsurge of implacable hatred, and these horrors and terror, for me, a Christian, writer and academic, to lose my illusions about our degree of humanity and our true level of civilization, we who give ourselves, without examination, for the best men in Central Africa."[37] Bishops, academics, Christians—no one escapes Ngoïe-Ngalla's diatribe. The author reproaches Christians and writers for their sterility. "It follows that, as Christians, we confess Christ only with our mouths and not with our hearts. It also follows that, like the fig tree in the Gospel, we are terribly barren Christians. And as writers, we are no less sterile, incapable

---

35. Djereke, "Mgr Albert Ndongmo, un prophète," 1.
36. Agenzia Fides, "'Nous sommes préoccupés.'"
37. Ngoïe-Ngalla, "Démission des hommes de prière," 366.

as we still are, for want of the necessary background, of helping men to change their lives, to reclaim themselves as living consciences with a vocation to the eternal and transcendent."[38] To the bishops, the author blames their pusillanimity. "I have no doubt that, draped in dazzling dalmatics, mitred like pharaohs of ancient Egypt and leading a silent demonstration . . . , our bishops would have produced, on a population so sensitive to the sacred and to the symbols of its expression, the most vivid impression that could have contained this unleashed fury and probably given the event another twist."[39] These words should serve as a flashlight for the whole of Congolese society, so that it never again falls into the same trap.

Another constructive criticism comes from Paulin Poucouta. He does it in a beautiful and evocative way. What Professor Poucouta (1996) says about the Church in Africa also applied to the Congo. "Despite its vitality, the Church in Africa is still fragile in many respects."[40] And he goes on to say that it is a "Church with bare hands, facing a gigantic task."[41] This mission of the Church, says the Congolese biblical scholar, is only possible if the Church has prophet-witnesses who are not soothsayers, but enlighteners, explorers of the future, in other words, clearers of the great uncultivated field that is Africa. The future of our countries in general, and the Congo in particular, is at stake.

With regard to the violence engendered by the management of natural resources, particularly oil, Congolese society could draw inspiration from what Poucouta wrote on violence. According to the author, violence is a monstrosity that must be rejected at all costs, a monstrosity that gives way to evil power exercised through violence. The Church in Africa, as an integral part of the historical community that is subjected to this violence, must play a major role in denouncing and combating it, thereby demonstrating its fidelity and love for the Lamb and the values he preaches. Hence

38. Ngoïe-Ngalla, "Démission des hommes de prière," 368.
39. Ngoïe-Ngalla, "Démission des hommes de prière," 369.
40. Poucouta, *Église dans la tourmente*, 36.
41. Poucouta, *Église dans la tourmente*, 36.

the development of a pastoral approach to peace[42] in the light of Revelation. This pastoral approach proposes an education that takes account of African wisdom and reality: our tales, our proverbs, our riddles, and so on. It's not enough to educate; we also need to inform: about how a society works, about democracy and human rights. Not only do we need to educate and inform, we also need to relearn how to accept each other as different, how to encourage action to combat violence, how to promote gestures of reconciliation between people in conflict, how to affirm gospel values: honesty, fidelity, courage, sharing, brotherhood. Then we can take on a therapeutic mission. It's our duty, it's the Church's duty. For, states Poucouta, "all these people traumatized by violence . . . need a psychological and spiritual detoxification cure."[43] Hence the need for absolute collaboration between churchmen and practitioners. This is also the perspective from which we can view the new evangelization. This evangelization, it should be remembered, also involves the actors of civil society.

How Does the Church in Congo Understand Her Sociological Function?

This section focuses on how the Congolese Church understands herself about her function. Such a function must be understood in a communal perspective, namely from the point of view of the Roman Catholic Church. In other words, the Congolese church understands her function within the reality of the Catholic Church as a whole. In such a case, it is not by chance that the Congolese Catholic Church finds the reason of her function within the discourse of the official church. That is, the Compendium of the Social Doctrine of the Church.

According to this compendium:

> The Church is not indifferent to what is decided, brought about or experienced in society; she is attentive to the

---

42. Poucouta, *Église dans la tourmente*, 104.
43. Poucouta, *Église dans la tourmente*, 106.

moral quality—that is, the authentically human and humanizing aspects—of social life. Society—and with it, politics, the economy, labour, law, culture—is not simply a secular and worldly reality, and therefore outside or foreign to the message and economy of salvation. Society in fact, with all that is accomplished within it, concerns man. Society is made up of men and women, who are "the primary and fundamental way for the Church."[44]

Indeed, what the Church in Congo has been doing until now corresponds to the spirit of the social doctrine of the church. It is obvious that this number 62 of the *Compendium of the Social Doctrine of the Church* implies the sociological function of the church. In it appears the idea of the church as a "social entity." For this reason, the church "is not indifferent to what is decided, brought about or experienced in society." In fact, it is by looking at what Congolese people experience that Bishop Louis Portella Mbuyu declares:

> The question of oil has been the object of a pastoral reflection on the part of the Church in Congo and the Church in Central Africa, considering the situation of great poverty that, paradoxically, characterizes the population living in this almost damned space where the black gold flows.[45]

This remark from the president of the Congolese Episcopal Conference provides a sociological critique of the Congolese society as well as the Central African region, where Congo is located. Thus, it is the fruit of a social analysis of the Congolese society. Such a remark must be understood in a context where the church understands the nature of her function, namely as a critic of society. Therefore, the church cannot be silent in countries where people live from hand to mouth.

In the words of Rahner, such a critique of the society by the church is not *ab externo*; "rather it is a critique from within, based

---

44. Conseil Pontifical Justice et Paix, *Compendium de la Doctrine Sociale*, 62.

45. Portella Mbuyu, "Insiste à temps," 4.

on the intrinsic tension within her between that which she herself seeks to be and that which she de facto is."⁴⁶ These Rahnerian words are relevant to the Congolese context because the church makes a critique of the Congo from within the Congolese society, as does Bishop Louis Portella Mbuyu as well as the other bishops of the Central African region, for the church knows the Congolese situation and tries to remain influential in the public realm of Congolese life.

In addition, the function of the church as a critic of society or as a "watchman" is not different from what is written in the declaration of the African bishops, *Ecclesia in Africa*, by Pope John Paul II. For the pope:

> Integral human development—the development of every person and of the whole person, especially of the poorest and most neglected in the community—is at the very heart of evangelization. Between evangelization and human advancement—development and liberation— there are in fact profound links. These include links of an anthropological order, because the man who is to be evangelized is not an abstract being but is subject to social and economic questions. They also include links in the theological order, since one cannot dissociate the plan of creation from the plan of Redemption. The latter plan touches the very concrete situations of injustice to be combatted and of justice to be restored. They include links of the eminently evangelical order, which is that of charity: how in fact can one proclaim the new commandment of love without promoting in justice and peace the true, authentic advancement of man?⁴⁷

These papal words define what might be understood as the "modus vivendi" of the Catholic Church towards the African society about social, economic, anthropological, and political matters.

This quotation above points to one of the most important aspects of the church's mission. First, the quotation indicates that working for the poorest and the most neglected is promoting

46. Rahner, "Function of the Church," 232.
47. John Paul II, *Ecclesia in Africa*, 68.

integral development. In other words, integral human development is the center of evangelization. Second, it makes clear that there is a profound relationship between evangelization, human advancement, development, and liberation, ranging from anthropological and theological orders to evangelical order. The theological order encompasses two different plans: creation and redemption. It is in the plan of redemption that issues of justice[48] and injustice are treated. Finally, charity is part of the evangelical order that also deals with love.

Indeed, taking care of the poor is a very old task in the church. For example, Saint Paul in his time encouraged Christians to help the poor.[49] As Stephen Bevans and Roger Schroeder put it, "Down through the ages the church has been noted for its care of the poor and those on the margins of society, and this has always been seen as part of the church's missionary outreach."[50]

However, over time, things changed. The church realized that caring for the poor and the most neglected was not enough for several reasons. The first reason was due to new understandings of human dignity and equality born of the Enlightenment.[51] The second reason was related to the "systemic causes of poverty in socialist and Marxist thought." The third and last reason was "the shift of the center of gravity of Christianity from the wealthy North to the poor South."[52]

These reasons have given new impetus to the mission of the Church, namely, to eradicate the roots of suffering and human exclusion. It is in this context that the concept of social justice reached its full extent because "the kingdom of God and social justice should not be separated."[53]

---

48. Justice as it appears it the Latin formulation, "*Suum cuique tradere*" translated as "to render to each what is his due." See Calvez, *Faith and Justice*, 73; Schroeder, "What of Mission," 117.

49. See Rom 16: 24–28; 1 Cor 16:1; Gal 2:10.

50. Bevans and Schroeder, "Justice, Peace and the Integrity," 369.

51. Bevans and Schroeder, "Justice, Peace and the Integrity," 370.

52. Bevans and Schroeder, "Justice, Peace and the Integrity," 369.

53. Bevans and Schroeder, "Justice, Peace and the Integrity," 369.

It is also in this context that we must understand the action of the bishops of Congo who show their solidarity with the poor and the neglected. Those bishops struggle to eradicate poverty and human exclusion. That is why they also want oil revenues to benefit the poor and, above all, all the Congolese people. This is the anthropological order that includes economic and social issues.[54] Effectively, in Congo, oil is a social[55] and an economic[56] issue.

Besides the anthropological order, there is also the theological order that includes the plan of creation and the plan of redemption. The human person is a divine creature, and he or she is part of God's plan of redemption. Indeed, the plan of redemption rejects any situation of injustice. As *Ecclesia in Africa* number 68 argues, injustice must be fought. In other words, the struggle of the Congolese bishops is a fight against injustice imposed on the Congolese people by irresponsible leaders. In such a situation a struggle for social justice becomes imperative.

Indeed, the struggle for social justice is very varied,[57] as has been said above.

Talking about justice is not only a matter of advocating on behalf of the poor and marginalized. It is also preaching peace among nations and peoples; as did in their time Gandhi, Martin Luther King, Bishop Romero, etc.[58] This means that our God is a God of justice and love as the church teaches us. In the words of Pedro Arrupe, "love being a condition for justice and justice being

---

54. Like any human being, the poor have needs to satisfy: for food, health care, clothing, housing, etc.

55. Because it involves men in society. There is even a popular adage that says, "in Congo, oil kills." See Secours Catholique, *Pour qui coule l'or noir?*, 3.

56. Congo has an industrial economy, that is, an economy in which industrial production represents the bulk of domestic production. See Grawitz, *Lexique des sciences sociales*, 142. Congo's economy is based particularly on the oil industry.

57. As Bevans and Schroeder put it, "The church's mission is intrinsically linked to its mission of cultivating and preserving peace among the peoples and nations in the world" ("Justice, Peace and the Integrity," 373).

58. Sobrino, "Monseñor Romero, a Salvadoran," 143–55; King, *Force d'aimer*, 15.

in the service of love."⁵⁹ Indeed, love mentioned here is the love of neighbor. "Love of neighbor and justice are inseparable. Love is above all a requirement of justice, that is, acknowledgment of the dignity and of the rights of one's neighbor."⁶⁰ The neighbor could be a believer or non-believer because God's justice deals with both. This is the good news that the church teaches us; a church which, according to Maritain, is seen differently by both believers⁶¹ and unbelievers.⁶² This is the evangelical order.

To sum up, it can be said that the Congolese Church understands her function in accordance with the social teaching of the church, in accordance with the spirit of Christ, and the understanding of the Congolese society.

After this section on how the Congolese church understands her function, it will be useful to focus on what the Congolese church says of the Congolese society.

---

59. Pedro Arrupe quoted by Calvez, *Faith and Justice*, 87.

60. Calvez, *Faith and Justice*, 131. See also World Synod of Catholic Bishops, *Justice in the world*.

61. As Maritain noted: "In the eyes of the unbeliever, the church is, or the churches are, organized bodies or associations especially concerned with the religious needs and creeds of a number of his fellow-men, that is, with spiritual values to which they have committed themselves, and to which their moral standards are appendant . . . Even though the unbeliever does not believe in these particular values, he has to respect them" (*Man and the State*, 150).

62. Maritain states that "for the believer the church is a supernatural society, both divine and human—the very type of perfect or achieved-in-itself, self-sufficient, and independent society—which unites in itself men as co-citizens of the kingdom of God and leads them to eternal life, already begun here below; which teaches them the revealed truth received in trust from the Incarnate Word Himself; which is the very body of which the head is Christ, a body visible, by reason of its essence, in its professed creed, its worship, its discipline and sacraments, and in the refraction of its supernatural personality through its human structure and activity, invisible in the mystery of the divine grace and charity vivifying human souls, even those which belong to that body without knowing it and only through the inner movement of explicit faith but seek God in truth" (*Man and the State*, 151).

The Catholic Church in Congo-Brazzaville

What Does the Church Say of the Congolese Society?

The church says many things about the Congolese society that deal with poverty, engagement in political affairs, and friendship between different ethnic groups, reconciliation, and respect for Christian principles.

The Congolese Church says that Congolese society is poor, but it doesn't deserve such poverty because Congo is a rich country. In other words, Congolese people must know that it is not normal to see more than 70 percent of their fellow countrymen living on less than one US dollar per day. By saying this, the Church wants Congolese society to be aware of its situation, and therefore it has the right to know the reason for such a situation. In fact, this is very relevant because the Church wants the Congolese society to be informed publicly on the management of the country by the politicians.

The Church thinks that Congolese believers as well as non-believers must be engaged in politics and not allow others to decide their future. This encouragement by the Church is somehow related to the previous point, because the Church, with the participation of Christians or honest people, could reduce the effect of mismanagement within the Congolese society.

The Church also promotes friendship between the different ethnic groups. In fact, in Congo, the ethnic argument is easily exploited by politicians when they want to divide the population. Thus, the Church wants Congolese people to be aware of this weakness that threatens harmony within the Congolese society. Unfortunately, the ethnic argument had the upper hand during the civil wars in the 1990s while politicians were fighting for the control of oil. That is why the Church insists on the virtue of reconciliation for Congolese society which is somehow divided.

Subsequently, the Church awakens the Congolese society to be aware of the ethical issues and helps Congolese people to decide what might be the role of social ethics in a divided society in which people mistakenly define their relationship according to their ethnic roots. This is contrary to Christian principles and therefore contrary to the teachings of Jesus.

In addition, the Catholic Church has attempted to show the Congolese people that, during the 1990s, they were misled by politicians who attempted to convince them that the civil wars experienced by the country were not ethnic confrontations. This was a deception by political leaders. Otherwise, to those who have been wrongly separated, injured psychologically, or divided falsely, the church proposes the virtue of unity and the strategy of reconciliation.[63]

As one might notice, this social discourse of the church towards the Congolese society is neither ignored nor misunderstood by the population. As a matter of fact, some Congolese politicians fear the views of some religious leaders.

Although the Congolese Catholic Church remains influential, she has seen some of her members put to death (martyrdom): Cardinal Emile Biayenda was assassinated in 1977, and some priests such as Benoit Gassongo, Jan Czuba, and Michel Halbecq, SJ, were executed in 1982 and 1998.

Besides this, the authority of the Catholic Church is recognized by other churches established in the country: Protestant, Muslim, and other Christian churches. Such a position strengthens the Catholic Church in Congo and allows her the right to intervene in social and political matters.

The Congolese Catholic Church as Seen by Congolese Society

For Congolese people, the Catholic Church is an important element of civil society. She is "the voice of the voiceless," and therefore one of the main institutions capable of speaking out or on behalf of the poor. The Church is the church of those who don't have voice because, during the democratic era, she put pressure on the government to allow a Sovereign National Conference by the Congolese people.

63. For more information see Daly and Sarkin, *Reconciliation in Divided Societies*, 10–16.

On the other hand, everywhere in Congo, people from different regions and from different generations have somehow understood the function the Congolese Church has to play in the matter of transparency in public matters. From this perspective such a function has been defined by Karl Rahner as "the function of the Church as a critic of society." Therefore, the Catholic Church in Congo cannot escape from such a function for the following reasons.

The Boundaries of the Church Are Not Outside the National Territory

Being part of a national territory, the Church is not foreign to what happens in the Congolese territory. In other words, she must be aware of not only what happens to the 42 percent of the population that claims to be Roman Catholics, but also to the entire Congolese population, including Protestants, Muslim, Kimbanguists, non-believers, etc.

A Leader of Opinion

Without engaging in politics, the Church must say what is important for the fellow Congolese to proclaim the message of Jesus Christ who came for believers as well as for non-believers. It is only by saying what she has to say for the general interest of Congolese people that the Church can be a leader of opinion. In fact, the Congolese Church has always been considered by the Congolese society as a leader of opinion, a counter-balance power, and an institution that inspires confidence. In other words, the Church is a church that inspires "responsibility" and "social engagement," and an institution that promotes peace, justice, and reconciliation.[64]

The church inspires confidence because during the democratic era she was chosen to lead the National Sovereign Conference.

---

64. For more information see Daly and Sarkin, *Reconciliation in Divided Societies*, 10–16; Schreiter, "Globalization and Reconciliation," 121–43.

The Role of the Congolese Catholic Church

During the armed conflicts of the 1990s, the church was also involved in the process of peace and reconciliation.

The church has also been considered as the church that provides "much needed humanitarian aid, moral comfort and a resemblance of security." In fact, on many occasions the civil population fleeing armed conflicts found refuge in churches, considered as neutral sanctuary areas, where they could find peace and spiritual and material support. In the words of Séraphin Ngouma, "The Church has also been the last bastion against those involved in the fighting. Politicians themselves have relied on the Church to address and regain the trust of the people, victims of armed conflicts for which only the politicians were responsible."[65]

All these considerations do not imply that Congolese people are totally satisfied with the Church's action; for they "need Church action to be more assertive."[66] In other words, they want the Church to be herself. This remark must be understood in its context. During the civil war in 1993–94, many Christians killed other Christians or non-believers. Bishops, priests, laity did nothing to stop such atrocity. Thus, it is not by chance that some Christians want a more assertive Church. Besides, such a remark might be understood as a reproach made by Christians regarding some of their bishops who seem to them to be too close to some politicians.[67] For the Church does not possess the same type of legitimacy as politicians do. In consequence, the Church must remain that social critic she is called to be. According to Yvon Christian Elenga, "In the eyes of Congolese people, the Catholic Church does not possess the same legitimacy as civil authorities to speak on public matters . . . In confronting many different and dangerous situations, the Congolese Church has assumed the role of social critic."[68] Concretely, it is only by retaining her role of social critic that one can understand the theological discourse of the Catholic Church in Congo. Indeed, if there is a theological discourse

---

65. Ngouma, "Responsibility of the Church," 12.
66. Ngouma, "Responsibility of the Church," 12.
67. On this subject see Bayart, "Églises chrétiennes et la politique," 3–26.
68. Elenga, "Congolese Church," 252.

The Catholic Church in Congo-Brazzaville

specifically held by the Catholic Church in Congo, such a discourse does not differ from the discourse held by the Catholic Church in the region of Central Africa. Such is the purpose of the next section.

Theological Discourse of the Catholic Church

The discourse of the Catholic Church in Congo is not markedly different from the other churches of Central Africa. The church's discourse is biblical and theological.

The discourse of the Church is based in the first place on the Scriptures. Congolese bishops as well as those from the Central African region say that "before the exploitation and the misery of the people, God rose up to say, 'I have seen the misery of my people and I have decided to free them.'"[69] For the bishops, "this liberating God has concern for all the oppressed of the world."[70] According to the bishops, God has seen the misery of his people from the Central African region. He wants to liberate them; this is his mission. In that mission God was followed by Jesus Christ, who announced the liberation of the oppressed of the world. Such a mission was given by Jesus to his disciples, the bishops who write on behalf of the people from the Central African region.

At the same time, the bishops also think that "our God is a God of union."[71] This unity is the symbol of God's solidarity. For them, "God united himself with the people he liberated and led them towards the land of happiness." That is, people who experience God's solidarity must also experience happiness in the land God gave to them. Such a land, say the bishops, must also be a land where the people of God experience values such as dignity, truth, justice, sharing, and solidarity.

In addition, the discourse of the bishops from the Central African region is also a theological discourse, based on the social

---

69. ACERAC, *Church and Poverty in Central Africa: Case of Oil*, 7.
70. ACERAC, *Church and Poverty in Central Africa: Case of Oil*, 7.
71. ACERAC, *Church and Poverty in Central Africa: Case of Oil*, 7.

teachings of the Roman Catholic Church. For, "the Church's tradition continues through the teachings of the Church fathers and the successors of Saint Peter."[72] In other words, aware of being successors of Saint Peter, and aware of their responsibility, the bishops want to be part of the Church's tradition. That is why they made the following principles part of the Church's social teachings in relation to natural resources, including oil.

These are the main principles:

- The universal destination of earthly goods: this principle is based on *Gaudium et Spes* 69: "God meant the earth and all it contains for the use of all human beings. This is why humans, in the use they make of it, must never hold the things they legitimately possess as belonging to them, but to regard them also as common in the sense they can profit not only owners, but others."
- The preferential option for the poor.
- The commitment to justice and peace.
- Solidarity among all human beings.
- The presence of the Church in the world.[73]

The Congolese bishops as well as those from the Central African region agreed on these principles to denounce corruption and embezzlement. Against corruption and embezzlement, two members of Congolese civil society, Brice Makosso and Christian Mounzeo, known for their courage and engagement, insisted that the government publish oil revenues. This was the purpose of their campaign *"Publiez ce que vous payez"* ("Publish What You Pay"), an international campaign against corruption and embezzlement of African oil by petroleum corporations and some African leaders with the complicity of Western countries.

---

72. ACERAC, *Church and Poverty in Central Africa: Case of Oil*, 8.
73. ACERAC, *Church and Poverty in Central Africa: Case of Oil*, 7.

The Possible Role of the Congolese Catholic Church

> "To understand the Congolese Church's role in promoting democracy, one must first understand the process whereby the Church accepted its new role as political agent."
>
> YVON CHRISTIAN ELENGA, SJ

The Church remains influential not only in the lives of believers, but also in the lives of non-believers who are aware of the role that the Church can play in the Congolese society.

In addition, the Church herself knows what role to play in society. This is understandable when, as Laurent Monsengwo Pasinya puts, "We as the Church have our own particular role to play. As Christians we cannot escape from the responsibility to analyze the context in which we are living, and fulfil our Christian duties which arise from that."[74] These words by the late archbishop of Kinshasa are true for the Congo for the main reason that the Catholic Church is universal. That is why, from what has been said above, it is possible to define what might be the possible role for the Church in Congo.

In this section, I advocate for a possible role for the Catholic Church in the Congolese society that can help to construct a positive social ethics. Congo being a country divided socially and politically, many questions arise regarding the possible role of religion in a rich country where corruption, mismanagement of natural resources, and rising poverty are prevalent.

In what follows, I suggest a reflection on the Congolese Catholic Church to explore the potential role of the Church in this country of the Central African region. By the notion "role of the Church," I mean what the Church does and how it functions in people's life using a functional definition of religion; religion being understood as a set of beliefs, rituals, and community experiences.

---

74. Quoted by McDonald, *Transparency*, 4. See also Fuellenbach, "Church in the context of the kingdom of God," 221–37.

The Role of the Congolese Catholic Church

As mentioned above, the Catholic Church in Congo has engaged in advocacy and action in favor of transparency in the use of petroleum revenues. The fact that Congolese bishops raised the question of the management of oil in a pastoral letter was a courageous witness to be taken into consideration for the future of the relationship between the Church and the state and between the Catholic Church and the Congolese society.

In addition, such a role must be effective in terms of efficacy and pragmatism. The Catholic Church in Congo must make this her modus vivendi towards ethical issues. In other words, the Catholic Church has been reflecting on her own role. If oil has been exploited in Congo since 1972, how can one understand the fact that it was only in the 1990s that the Catholic Church engaged herself in the public sphere? This might also encourage religious leaders to train Christians in the management of natural resources, and in issues related to human resources.

There are two ways one can interpret the possible role of the Catholic Church in Congo. The first way deals with the role of being well informed. In other words, the Church must know herself what is going on in the Congolese public sphere. It is only by being informed that she can know what to say to Congolese people. For example, being informed supposes knowing the role of being informed. Concretely, it is knowing where to find and how to use information. The second way deals with the necessity of informing the Congolese people. If the Church cannot inform the Congolese population, it means that she doesn't exist for the Congolese people. Therefore, she has to make herself visible by playing her role. As Peter Berger and Thomas Luckmann put it, "to say, then, that roles represent institutions is to say that roles make it possible for institutions to exist, ever again as a real presence in the experience of living individuals."[75]

From this brief survey, it can be said that the role of the Congolese Catholic Church is a role of being informed and informing. This entails being well informed on what happens in the Congolese public sphere and informing the Congolese population. For,

---

75. Berger and Luckmann, *Social Construction of Reality*, 75.

the population is calling on the Church to intervene to dress its wounds, to feed the hungry and the victims of violence resulting from the political and military crises. Above all the Congolese call upon the Church to take on more responsibility, beyond that of providing emergency aid, by working to defend human rights, argue for equality and justice, and fight against corruption and poverty. In truth, the Church must play the role of sentry, who foresees alerts, announces, but also denounces.[76]

This chapter focused on an important element of the civil society in Congo, which is the Catholic Church. First it provided a brief overview of the history of the Roman Catholic Church to understand it from a wider universal, continental perspective. The purpose of this procedure was not only to understand the interaction between the Congolese church and the hierarchical Church in terms of its evolution and the evangelization of the African continent as well as the evangelization of Congo, but also to see how the Church intervened in the public sphere by means of schools, hospitals, education, etc. This leads to an understanding of the function and role of the Church in Africa and therefore in Congo. Such a function has been understood as a critic of society according to Karl Rahner. From there, it was possible to understand the role of the Church in the Congolese society about its historicity and its challenges or duties for the future. This understanding of her role by the church is a prerequisite for understanding her own function. By doing so, the Church can say something coherent about the Congolese society and therefore build a biblical or a theological discourse with special emphasis on some principles relevant for the fabric of an ethical Congolese society. In return, the Congolese society can say what she expects from the Church, what the church does well or less well, determining her possible duties or challenges so as to be more effective in Congo. All this helps the Church to be aware of her function and therefore determine what her role might be in the Congolese society.

---

76. Ngouma, "Responsibility of the Church," 13. Ellis and Ter Haar, *Worlds of power: Religious Thought*.

The Role of the Congolese Catholic Church

This chapter raises several issues such as the promotion of social justice related to politics; how the Church's role within Congo is linked with it being part of a global institution; and how the principles of universal destination of earthly goods, the preferential option for the poor, the commitment to justice and peace, solidarity among all human beings as well as the presence of the Church in the world can be grounded theologically and perhaps also in philosophy. These issues are worthy of discussion.

As a matter of fact, a sound understanding of the notion of the common good is relevant to the promotion of a social and economic justice in the Congo. Indeed, a good management of the common good is a prerequisite for a more ethical Congo and therefore a more positive transformative praxis in the Congolese ethos. This is the purpose of the next chapter.

THREE

African Ethics and Management of the Common Good

in Promoting Social and Economic Justice in Relation to Oil

THIS CHAPTER SHOWS THE importance of social ethics in managing the common good and promoting economic and social justice. Hence the use of African ethics according to Bujo, the place of the common good in the Congolese Constitution, not forgetting the importance of an ethical and social discourse to mark out the path, drawing on several authors (Sacks, Maritain, Thomas Aquinas). It should also be stressed that the advent of economic and social justice in connection with oil necessarily requires respect for the human person, ethical standards for economic life, and moral priorities for the nation: sine qua non conditions for a better way of living together.

In the following, I start from some ideas based on African ethic and then will build an analysis around the notion of the common good with respect to social and economic justice in Congo. I contend that social and economic justice is an ethical issue in a sense that ethics is about individual action as well as the action of public institutions. Concretely, ethics has a social dimension as well as a collective dimension often linked to politics.[1]

My aim is threefold. First, I present an African ethic according to Bénézet Bujo (1940–2023) with a special emphasis on the significance of the community.[2] My focus is to understand the reasons behind this difference between the African ethic that gives primacy to the community and the difficulty in managing the common good intended to serve the whole community. Is this a problem of political strategy or just a problem of political will? I will answer this question later.

My second aim is to look at what has been done[3] and what needs to be done[4] to help the Congo to move forward. My focus here is to know why and how Congo-Brazzaville needs to develop an ethical discourse based on a procedural method of ethical analysis that implies both the management of the common good[5] and a culture of social and economic justice. To do this, an understanding of the concept of common good is fundamental. I will do this in two steps, first using a few excerpts from the Congolese Constitution, and then calling upon a few specialists who deserve our attention: Jacques Maritain, Jonathan Sacks, and Thomas Aquinas.

My last point concerns the notion of economic and social justice. The goal is to see how this concept works with the notion of common good. On this point, I will rely on the pastoral letter *Economic Justice for All* by the US bishops. My interest in this letter involves how it shows the American Catholic Church has

---

1. All that is social is likely to become political in the sense that, animated by powerful social groups, it brings a reaction of power and integrates this in the political game (J. Leca). See Grawitz, *Lexique des sciences sociales*, 318. As Aristotle states, "The science that studies the supreme good for man is politics" (*Nichomachean Ethics*, lv); Gavric and Sienkiewicz, *Etat et bien commun*, 1–4.

2. This should in fact be an argument to facilitate social and economic justice for all Congolese.

3. With respect to social and economic justice, since Congo is an oil-producing country.

4. One must keep in mind all oil-related conflicts that Congo experienced in the 1990s.

5. Mainly, oil.

built her analysis on issues[6] of social and economic justice that can help other churches around the world, including the Congolese Church.

The argument of this chapter is that the political management of the common good cannot ignore ethics. I also contend that the management of the common good depends on how we understand the territory in which that common good is located. This is my approach in addressing the problem of the management of the common good with special attention to the oil produced in Congo.

African Traditional Ethic: Significance of the Community (the Contribution of Bénézet Bujo)

Why start this chapter with an ethical concern? My answer to this question is that to talk about social and economic issues is somehow to deal with human communities. As in most sub-Saharan African countries, much importance is given to the community. Given that it is the community that is concerned, I find it plausible to start with African ethics in which much significance is given to the community.

I present some highlights from Bujo's books on African ethic, namely, *Foundations of an African Ethic: Beyond the Universal Claims of Western Morality*.[7] The choice of this book is justified by the fact that I want to understand the role that is played by ethics in African politics. From this book I only touch on a few key ideas.

It is worth mentioning that over the last twenty years there has been great interest in the quest for an African ethics. Many African theologians have tried to identify the fundamental question of African ethics. Among them is Bénézet Bujo,[8] who believes

---

6. This is an example to the world since many local Catholic churches—including the Congolese Catholic Church—now look to the example of the American Catholic Church to lobby their respective governments through the US Congress on issues of social and economic justice.

7. Bujo, *Foundations of an African Ethic*; Bujo, *Ethical Dimension of Community*, 1–132; O'Neill, "African Moral Theology," 123–39.

8. A priest of the diocese of Bunia, in the Democratic Republic of Congo

that there is a definite European ethic as well as an African ethic. For example, in European thought the individual human person is acknowledged as the starting point, while in the African context primacy is given to the visible and invisible community.[9]

Moreover, Bujo thinks that "African ethic seeks no self-legitimation. It accepts the confrontation with other ethical systems because it hopes for a reciprocal give and take that can enrich both sides."[10]

Indeed, it is important to mention that an African ethics is open to other types of ethics. That is why I will call upon non-African authors in the second part of this chapter to see how the Congo can enrich its understanding of the common good.

In addition, Bujo discusses the fundamental questions of African ethic: community, deceased ancestors, God, palaver, etc. For this author, *"Africans tend in practice to speak about human beings rather than about God; this is due to the view that one who pays heed to the dignity of the human person also pleases God, and that one who acts against the human person offends precisely this God."*[11] This is a peculiarity of the negro-African thought that is based on the human being.

However, regarding the management of oil in Congo, the dignity of the human person has not been respected in different situations, probably due to the interests of some politicians.[12] This lack of respect for human dignity has caused a lot of reaction, especially on the part of bishops who assert that:

> The Congolese people do not know much about how much our country receives from this black gold, and even less about how the revenues are managed. What it does know is the price of oil is measured not in barrels,

---

(DRC); professor of moral theology and ethics at the University of Fribourg (Switzerland), and an expert in African theology. He passed away on November 9, 2023.

9. Bujo, *Foundations of an African Ethic*, 1.
10. Bujo, *Foundations of an African Ethic*, iv.
11. Bujo, *Foundations of an African Ethic*, 2; italics added.
12. Interests related to oil revenues.

or dollars but in suffering, misery, successive wars, blood, displacement of people, exile, unemployment, late payment of salaries, non-payment of pensions.[13]

These words by the Congolese bishops show that oil revenues are not well distributed and economic justice as well as social justice is practically nonexistent in Congo.

There are two principles in African ethic that deserve my attention: the importance given to the community and the respect of human dignity. These principles are very important for our reflection because they allow us to understand the relationship between the Congolese politicians and their fellow citizens and the relationship that the Congolese politicians have with things such as oil, money, wealth, etc. This shows that the Congolese politicians attach little importance to African ethics.

This leads me to raise some questions. How can we explain that 70 percent of the population lives below the poverty line while the country produces oil daily? How are we to understand that in an African society, the good of the community is no longer a concern?

Two possible cases: either there is a total neglect of African principles of ethics, or there is a lack of interest on the part of politicians. I will affirm this later even though there is no doubt that there is a problem.

The problem is that while the Congo continues to produce oil, some politicians get rich at the expense of the Congolese people. They usually mix politics with things that have nothing to do with politics. As Patrick Chabal and Jean-Pascal Daloz put it:

> Politics is seen legitimately to include many other, less obviously political, activities. Perhaps the most fluid in this respect is that which links political and economic enterprise. In Africa, it is expected that politics will lead to personal enrichment just as it is expected that wealth will have direct influence on political matters. Rich men

---

13. Évêques du Congo, "Pétrole et la mission," 2–4.

are powerful. Powerful men are rich. Wealth and power are inextricably linked.[14]

This poses another problem, that of the elusive nature of the relationship that exists between politics and economics in many African countries, including Congo. Indeed, the relationship of men to things is not very clear in Congo where some politicians are also businessmen. The problem is that they become businessmen thanks to oil money. It is this relationship of humans to things that explains why the Congolese population is reduced to poverty[15] while oil can change the lives of most of the Congolese people. There is something to be learned from this situation.

What can we learn from Bujo regarding the management of oil? Given that the African ethic is based on anthropology, the human being should be at the center of the management of the common good. In the Congolese case, it is quite the opposite, since the work of man is set aside in favor of a small group. This leads me to think that there is a loophole regarding compliance of African ethics in Congo. What then explains the difference between African ethic (based on anthropology) and politics?

Apropos of African ethics Bujo says that "the person is not defined as an ontological act by means of self-realization, but by means of 'relations.'"[16] Relations are illustrated in Bujo's book by proverbs. Bujo gives several examples by demonstrating the important role of proverbs in African life. For example, the proverb "Human beings did not come out of a tree or a stick" emphasizes the importance of relationships and solidarity inside the community.

Through this example, I want to show that the management of oil can be approached in an ethical-African perspective. Such a perspective attributes a significant role to the palaver. The role of the palaver shows that "ethical responsibility is the common work

14. Chabal and Daloz, *Africa Works*, 52. See also Bratton and Van de Walle, *Democratic Experiments in Africa*.

15. Secours Catholique, *Congo-Brazzaville*, 3–20; Tonda, "Guerre dans le 'camp Nord,'" 50–67.

16. Bujo, *Foundations of an African Ethic*, 88. Unfortunately, there are related accomplices who go against the well-being of the population.

of the community."[17] This ethical responsibility motivates my investigation of the problem of oil in Congo.

Management of oil is not the case of one Congolese; on the contrary it is the responsibility of all Congolese. In other words, it is a matter that concerns all humans who promote justice and peace in the world and therefore in Congo.

In addition, "the individual cannot avoid reflecting on how his ethical actions affect the community."[18] That is why those who have responsibility for managing oil in Congo must ask themselves questions about the consequences of their actions at the national level.

Bujo's book has two merits: the first is that it offers a look at African morality, especially Bantu. The second is that it helps both African and non-African people to understand African ethic in an African context. Such understanding is necessary especially when it comes to the management of the common good in any given African community.

The management of oil is indeed a matter for the community. If I have entitled this reflection *The Role of the Congolese Church*, it is also because it relates to the Congolese society. Indeed, when one wants to promote something, it is assumed that this promotion somehow does not exist yet. This also means that social and economic justice is not yet a reality in Congo.[19]

Congo has been an oil-producing country since 1972. This leads me to raise some questions. How is it then that for fifty-two years, economic and social justice are not yet a reality? How can we understand that in an African country where the notion of community is very strong, there are problems regarding the management of oil, which is a common good? Have Congolese politicians lost the value of the concept of the common good? How then do we understand that the Congo, which is the fifth-largest oil producer in Africa, is still a poor country? How can one explain to the

---

17. Bujo, *Foundations of an African Ethic*, 125.
18. Bujo, *Foundations of an African Ethic*, 125.
19. Even if there has been progress, much remains to be done.

70 percent of Congolese who live below the poverty line that their country makes profits from oil exports?

These are questions relevant to this reflection. My impression is that there is a real problem in terms of "understanding" the concept of common good. This is due to the inability of the Congolese politicians to manage the common good and promote social and economic justice. Have they forgotten that the common good is primarily for the largest number?

This failure is probably due to an impoverishment of the concept of the common good among our politicians. Even if the concept of the common good is somehow present in the Congolese Constitution, our politicians do little to promote social and economic justice. However, it would be interesting to see how the Congolese Constitution refers to the common good. This brings us to the next section.

The Notion of the Common Good

This section is divided into two parts. The first relates to the common good in the Congolese Constitution. The second part addresses the common good as viewed by Jonathan Sacks, Jacques Maritain, and Thomas Aquinas.

The Common Good and the Congolese Constitution

What relationship exists between the Congolese Constitution and the common good? To answer this question, I will refer to the Preamble that states:

> *We, the Congolese People*
> *Declare our determination to build a rule of law and a nation of fraternity and solidarity;*
> *Condemn the coup d'état, the tyrannical exercise of power and the use of political violence in all its forms as a means of accessing power or preservation; Adhere to universal values of peace, freedom, equality, justice, tolerance,*

> *honesty and the virtues of dialogue, as cardinal points of the new political culture;*
> *Reaffirm the sanctity of human life, property rights and the right to be different; Reaffirm solemnly our inalienable right to permanent sovereignty over all our wealth and our natural resources as a fundamental element of our development;*
> *Declare an integral part of this Constitution the principles proclaimed and guaranteed by:*
> - *the United Nations Charter of 24 October 1945;*
> - *the Universal Declaration of Human Rights of 10 December 1948;*
> - *the African Charter on Human and Peoples' Rights of 26 June 1981;*
> - *all relevant international instruments duly ratified and relating to human rights;*
> - *the Charter of National Unity and the Charter of Rights and Freedoms adopted by the Sovereign National Conference May 29, 1991;*
>
> *Ordain and establish, for Congo, this Constitution establishes the basic principles of the Republic, defines the rights and duties of citizens and establishes the organizational forms and operating rules of the state.*[20]

With respect to the use of national resources, when we look at this Preamble, it seems that only a few lines allude implicitly to the common good, namely, "we reaffirm solemnly our inalienable right to permanent sovereignty over all our wealth and our natural resources as a fundamental element of our development." It is expressly made clear that natural resources are earmarked for development. Basically, the concept of common good is not very explicit. One can legitimately ask why.

Indeed, during my many stays in Congo, I have noticed that the Congolese society suffers from many problems. One of those problems, for example, is a lack of a social, ethical, and pragmatic discourse to promote social and economic justice.

---

20. Translated from French into English by the author. République du Congo, *Constitution du 20 janvier 2002*, "Préambule."

THE ROLE OF THE CONGOLESE CATHOLIC CHURCH

In addition, Congolese people feel that while the money comes in, they do not know where it goes. It seems that some individuals get richer, while the country becomes poorer and poorer.

I think that we need to rethink the management of the common good. This "management" should involve both the creation of the common good and its distribution to all the Congolese people.

Theoretically, oil brings money home, but that money does not serve the entire population. We might ask whether this is since the concept of common good does not permeate the minds of our leaders, or if it is a question of political will. The second possibility seems to outweigh the first, even if the first possibility is also plausible. But to avoid drawing hasty conclusions, I would like to look at the concept of common good through the intermediary of some authors. This is the purpose of the following section.

The Need for a Social and Ethical Discourse

I will begin with Jonathan Sacks and focus on chapter 2 of his book *The Home We Build Together* (2007). This chapter can be helpful because it offers a clearer idea about how a country can be built as a home by all its citizens. In the Congolese case, how can diverse ethnic groups engage each other in dialogue about the management of the common good in relation to politics?

FOLLOWING JONATHAN SACKS

Thinking especially of the management of the common good, certain authors deserve particular attention. Jonathan Sacks, for example, uses a beautiful image for the construction of a social ethics based on the use of the common good as a "home we build together." The concrete links between Sacks's second chapter and the Congolese situation are: inevitable diversity (essential to political life); the common engagement in society-building; "home," "build" (a focus on responsibilities, rights, contributions, and claims); society; virtues and values.

Ethnically, Congo-Brazzaville has about sixty ethnic groups, spread over the fifteen departments[21] that make up the country. If the results from oil are not being distributed to ALL the people but benefit only a few, it means that Congo-Brazzaville is not a home for ALL the Congolese people. To be considered as a home, Congo-Brazzaville must be seen—following Sacks's interpretation—as a society that is not a house, nor a hotel, but a home. I borrow this image (a home we build together) from Sacks, whose interpretation is based on three parables in which a hundred strangers "have been wandering around the countryside in search of a place to stay." As a result, the owner comes to the gate, speaks with them and asks them to stay as long as they can. The problem here is that the strangers are guests. This is society as country house (first parable). Applied to Congo-Brazzaville, this parable is not helpful because Congolese people cannot be considered guests in their own country.

The second parable is neither interesting nor helpful because it considers "a hundred strangers in search for a home [who] find themselves in the middle of a big city" where they find a hotel and stay. As a matter of fact, their relationship with the hotel is "purely contractual" because "they pay money in return for certain services." This is not possible for the construction of a social and ethical discourse in Congo-Brazzaville. Such a discourse must deal with the third parable in which "a hundred strangers arrive at a town" and meet the mayor, councilors, and local residents who accept to welcome them without accommodation and help them to build homes. As Jonathan Sacks puts it: "the homes they build are recognizably of the place where they are, not the place they are from. Not only have they made a home; they have made themselves at home, in this landscape, this setting, this place."[22]

This third parable does not involve the conditions of paying as in a hotel, nor having a contractual agreement. It is based on

---

21. Kouilou, Niari, Bouenza, Lékoumou, Pool, Plateaux, Cuvette, Cuvette-Ouest, Sangha, Likouala, Brazzaville, and Pointe-Noire. Three new departments since July 3, 2024: Nkeni-Alima, Djoué-Léfini and Congo-Oubangui.

22. Sacks, *Home We Build Together*, 14.

The Role of the Congolese Catholic Church

a serious commitment, a shared project, a modus vivendi, and a friendship. "That is society as the home we build together." That is Congo-Brazzaville as I would like it to be: a society that belongs to ALL the Congolese people.

The concept of "society" as Jonathan Sacks puts it "is where we come together to achieve collectively what none of us can do alone. It is our common property. We inhabit it, make, and breathe it. It is the realm in which all of us is more important than any one of us. It is our shared project, and it exists to the extent that we work for it and contribute to it."[23]

This definition, even if it is not a scientific one, has the merit of giving an idea of society as something that is constructed by people who live in it, not only the nationals, but also the immigrants. This is why I would like to understand the Congolese society as something constructed by Congolese as well as non-Congolese people who live in the territory of Congo-Brazzaville.

Following Maritain

Another author I think helpful is Jacques Maritain with his book *The Person and the Common Good*.[24] I will mainly focus on chapter 3, "Individuality and Personality," and chapter 4, "The Person and Society."

In chapter 3, Maritain states that there is a metaphysical distinction between individuality and personality. Here, the French philosopher uses an analogy regarding Thomistic personalism. For Maritain, the human being is divided into two poles: a material pole (individuality) and a spiritual pole (personality).

In terms of our reflection, this division is important for two reasons. The first reason is that the common good is related to the concept of personality as that of individuality. It is important to say that for Maritain, the common good is not an individual

---

23. Sacks, *Home We Build Together*, 5.
24. Maritain, *Person and the Common Good*, 50–80.

property or a collection of individual properties.[25] In other words, the common good is interested in the human person and not in the individual. This means that the common good is primarily concerned with the social dimension of the human person.[26] This distinction is important because it shows that the common good is interested in the welfare of all Congolese and not the interests of some individuals who merely want to get rich on oil money. It is understandable why Maritain was opposed to a liberalism that denies the social dimension of the human person. The second reason is that the concept of individuality deals with matter whereas the concept of personality deals with the deepest and highest dimension of being. Maritain understands the concept of personality as a subsistence of the spiritual soul communicated to the human composite. It means interiority to self.[27]

What Maritain wants to demonstrate is the fact that personality and individuality are not separate. Individual derives from matter while person derives from spirit. Personality tends by nature to communion visible in social communications, education, and the help of other men.

The concrete links between these chapters and the situation in Congo are determined by the fact that we are confronted with the distinction between individuality and personality. This point can be helpful regarding the problem of corruption, justice, and love towards the others or the neighbors. Since the management of the common good also deals with virtues such as justice and love, it is important to mention that when Maritain speaks of virtue, conscience, and law as being part of the common good, he is speaking of some of the moral conditions needed if resources such as oil are really to benefit ALL. His use of terms such as *virtue* and

---

25. Friboulet, "Bien commun selon Jacques Maritain," 2.

26. Friboulet, "Bien commun selon Jacques Maritain," 2. According to David Hollenbach, "Maritain's position can be called personalist communitarianism, for its central anthropological affirmation is 'that personality tends by nature to communion'" ("Common Good Revisited," 85); see Brueggemann, *Journey to the Common Good*, 20–100.

27. Maritain, *Person and the Common Good*, 41.

conscience imply that this is a moral issue, not just an economic issue.

Chapter 4 of *The Person and the Common Good* can be helpful in considering the place of the person in society or the place of the Congolese citizen in the wider community.[28] Indeed, according to Maritain society is not secondary. Society is an essential condition for the flourishing of the person.[29] As Maritain puts it, "the common good is common because it is received in persons, each one of whom is a mirror of the whole."[30] For Maritain, society has an end. "The end of society is the good of the community, of the social body."[31] Indeed, there is no society without common good. "If the good of the social body is not understood to be a common good of human persons . . . this conception also would lead to other errors of a totalitarian type."[32] In the eyes of Maritain, to disregard the common good leads to totalitarianism. In other words, in addition to liberalism, Maritain also refutes totalitarianism. The common good is not unique to the whole and thus to the state he represents.[33]

For Maritain, the common good goes with ethics, justice, etc. "The common good is something ethically good. Included in it, as an essential element, is the maximum possible development, here and now, of the persons making up the united multitude to the end of forming people, organized not by force alone but by justice."[34]

These words, drafted in the twentieth century, are valid today in the twenty-first century, including in Congo. In other words, the Congo can be inspired by Maritain to help the Congo to advance. These are ideas that may be useful to the management of the common good in the Congo. In addition to Maritain, the Congo can also learn from Thomas Aquinas.

28. For more information see Maritain, *Man and the State*, 19–151.
29. Friboulet, "Bien commun selon Jacques Maritain," 2.
30. Maritain, *Man and the State*, 49.
31. Maritain, *Man and the State*, 50.
32. Maritain, *Man and the State*, 50.
33. Friboulet, "Bien commun selon Jacques Maritain," 3.
34. Maritain, *Person and the Common Good*, 53–54.

African Ethics and Management of the Common Good Following Thomas Aquinas

Another author that merits my attention is Thomas Aquinas. This author has an interesting perspective regarding the management of the common good. For him, the common good deals with the virtuous life of the citizens.

Thomas Aquinas's interpretation of the common good is important in its analogical nature. As he puts it:

> It is impossible that a man be good, unless he be well ordered to the common good, nor can the whole be well ordered unless its parts be proportioned to it. Consequently, the common good of the state cannot flourish, unless the citizens be virtuous, at least those whose business it is to govern. But it is enough for the good of the community that the other citizens be so far virtuous that they obey the commands of their rulers.[35]

A good and realistic social and ethical discourse needs virtuous citizens in the case of Congo-Brazzaville to make it a "home we build together."

In addition, the common good has a theological connotation in Thomas Aquinas. As David Hollenbach puts it, "For Thomas, the full common good is God's will. Human beings achieve their ultimate fulfillment, their good, only by being united with God, a union that unites them to one another and indeed with the whole created order."[36]

It is interesting that the notion of common good is related to the concept of God. Consequently, it is also linked to the concept of the human person. As Maritain puts it:

> Because the common good is the human common good, it includes within its essence . . . the service of the human person. The adage of the superiority of the common good is understood in its true sense only in the measure

---

35. Aquinas (1a2ae, 92.1 ad 3) quoted by Hollenbach, "Common Good Revisited," 81.

36. Hollenbach, "Common Good Revisited," 81.

that the common good itself implies a reference to the human person.[37]

This reminds me of what has been said about the African anthropology, that is, to do good to man is to do good to God. In other words, following Thomas Aquinas, God is not honored when the common good does not benefit the Congolese people.

Considering the positions of Bujo, Sacks, Maritain, and Thomas Aquinas, how can we build a social and economic ethics in the Congo? Such is the focus of the next section.

Social and Economic Justice in Relation to Oil

In this section, I will discuss the concepts of social and economic justice as they appear in the Congolese case in their relation to oil, for Congo's management of oil poses a real problem of social and economic justice.

Initially, I will give a definition of these two concepts linking them to the case of Congo. Then I will consider the pastoral letter of the American bishops *Economic Justice for All*.

Promote Social and Economic Justice in Congo

In this section, I will emphasize a few salient points involving the promotion of social and economic justice.

The concept of justice leads us to two other concepts: commutative justice and social justice. On the one hand, commutative justice is focused on individuals (equality of opportunity in the exchange) and on the other hand social justice is based on the notion of rendering to each according to his economic productivity or according to his functions, his responsibilities, rank, or needs.[38] I will focus more on the second type of justice, i.e., social justice.

The situation I have described in the previous chapters shows that no serious action promotes social and economic justice in

---

37. Maritain, *Person and the Common Good*, 29–30.
38. Grawitz, *Lexique des sciences sociales*, 248.

Congo for the simple reason that 70 percent of the Congolese people live below the poverty line.

In my opinion the Congo needs a good policy of social and economic justice. At least two reasons justify this. The first relates to the various conflicts that caused the country to mourn. Most of these conflicts were linked to oil. The second is related to the aggravation of poverty. As I said above, over 70 percent of the Congolese population lives below the poverty line.

In such a situation, we should strive to avoid the recurrence of past conflicts. But this is only possible if the Congolese have a constructive politics of social justice and economic justice. In addition, to have a sound economic and social policy is a guarantee for social peace. The recent events in the Arab world confirm this. But to achieve this social peace, some conditions are required.

In the present case of the Congo, an oil-producing country, it is necessary to focus on the dimensions of the economic life of the Congolese. As the US bishops state, "economy should be measured not only by what it produces, but also by whether it protects or undermines the dignity of the human person."[39]

This quote is important for the Congolese, because we see that the more oil the country produces, the poorer the Congolese become. This should be an indicator of social economic policy. It is abnormal that a country becomes rich while impoverishing its people.

Another important aspect in the pastoral letter of the American bishops is that "economic decisions have important moral dimensions: they can help or hurt people, strengthen or weaken families, and promote or diminish justice in our nation or world."[40]

This is very true in the case of Congo, where oil is seen as the cause of all our misfortunes because of the politicians who are more interested in controlling oil rather than the well-being of the Congolese. Such an approach is a failure of democracy and a resurgence of neo-patrimonialism. In other words, the problem is first and foremost political. As Patrick Chabal states:

39. U.S. Bishops, *Economic Justice for All*, v.
40. U.S. Bishops, *Economic Justice for All*, v.

> *Contemporary politics in Africa is best understood as the exercise of neo-patrimonialism power. What this means in concrete terms is that, despite the formal political structures in place, power is exercised essentially through the informal sector. Or rather, it is in the interplay between the formal and the informal that the kernel of politics is to be found on the continent.*[41]

What Chabal says is not different from the words of the US bishops because economic decisions are taken in politics. And, consequently, the issue must be seen as a function of politics since it is the politicians who have the decision power. However, the problem is deeper than it appears. According to Chabal, "*this form of government (namely neo-patrimonialism) rests on well understood, if unequal, forms of political reciprocity which links patrons with their clients along vertical social lines.*"[42] This leads us to the next section.

Following the US Bishops

My argument in this section is that the promotion of social and economic justice proceeds only through a good public policy. It requires that several conditions be met. I have listed some following the pastoral letter *Economic Justice for All*.

Respect of the Human Person

There is a fundamental condition that must be met in Congo to promote social and economic justice for the Congolese people. Quoting Pope John XXIII, the US bishops state that "the basis for all that the Church believes about the moral dimensions of economic life is its vision of the transcendent worth—the sacredness—of human beings. The dignity of the human person, realized

---

41. Chabal, "Quest for Good Government," 450; italics added.
42. Chabal, "Quest for Good Government," 450; italics added.

in the community with others, is the criterion against which all aspects of economic life must be measured."[43]

This condition also applies to Congo. It helps to understand a human person as a sacred being. Indeed, it should not be surprising since this is the same point that appears in the African ethics proposed by Bujo. Furthermore, it is a confirmation of what Maritain and Thomas Aquinas said of the human person. In other words, politics needs ethics.

Ethical Norms for Economic Life

Another aspect that I find important is the respect of ethical standards. This is very important because, according to the American bishops, it refers to the application of Christian norms in a pluralistic society. The Congo as a pluralistic society has duties to its citizens and vice versa. As the US bishops state:

> First we outline the duties all people have to each other and to the whole community: love of neighbor, the basic requirements of justice and the special obligation to those who are poor or vulnerable. Corresponding to these duties are the human rights of every person; the obligation to protect the dignity of all demands respect for these rights. Finally these duties and rights entail several priorities that should guide the economic choices of individuals, communities, and the nation as a whole.[44]

Though written in an American context, this applies also to the Congo if we consider the history of each country.

Moral Priorities for the Nation

This point is also important because it highlights the notion of the common good. As the US bishops say, "The common good

---

43. U.S. Bishops, *Economic Justice for All*, 31.
44. U.S. Bishops, *Economic Justice for All*, 41.

demands justice for all, the protection of the human rights of all."⁴⁵ Indeed, a common good which does not comply with justice for all is not a common good.

How does the common good relate to the principle of justice? In the words of Jean-Yves Calvez, the Second Vatican Council recognized "that large numbers of people had become 'clearly aware' of injustices and the 'unequal distribution' of this world's goods. Likewise, among nations there are tremendous inequalities, and gaps between the wealthy and poor only 'grow more and more.' Often, there is a kind of growth which seems to be unjust, characterized by 'dependence, even in the economic sphere' (no. 9.)."⁴⁶ The understanding of the connection between common good and justice is fundamental because there is no justice without common good. As David Hollenbach, SJ, would say, "justice is a prerequisite for a good that is common."⁴⁷ Such a connection can be seen in different perspectives: friendship, solidarity, as well as law. That is why "Aquinas held that all law should be directed to the promotion of the common good."⁴⁸ This interpretation creates a link of solidarity between common good and justice because "from a common good perspective . . . justice calls for the minimal level of solidarity required to enable all of society's members to live with basic dignity."⁴⁹ Indeed, with regard to the Congolese society, the Congolese people need their dignity to be respected. As members of the Congolese community, they want the community to be in solidarity with them because there is no justice without it and there is no common good without it. David Hollenbach explains it well when he states that "the norm of justice spells out the minimal requirements of solidarity that is a prerequisite for lives lived in

---

45. U.S. Bishops, *Economic Justice for All*, 46. See also Hollenbach, *Justice, Peace and Human Rights*, 19–88; Curran, *Catholic Moral Tradition Today*, 19–99; Badiou, *Metapolitics*, 106.

46. Calvez, *Faith and Justice*, 14.

47. Hollenbach, *Common Good*, 190.

48. Hollenbach, *Common Good*, 192.

49. Hollenbach, *Common Good*, 192.

dignity."⁵⁰ Indeed, by doing justice, the human being is directed toward what is good. That is why Thomas Aquinas believed that "the premier moral virtue is justice, which directs a person's actions toward the good of fellow human beings."⁵¹ This observation can be confirmed in commutative as well as distributive justice. That is why the US bishops believe that general justice or contributive justice "spells out the contribution to the common good that justice requires from individual people."⁵² In relating this latter term to the case of oil in Congo, it can be inferred that the common good deals absolutely with distributive justice because "the good of the community should set the direction for the lives of individuals for it is a higher or more 'divine' good than the particular goods of private persons."⁵³ These words by Aristotle confirm Thomas Aquinas's statement when he says that "God's own self is the highest good we can attain, and that a right to God requires a commitment to the common good of our neighbors and of all creation."⁵⁴ Indeed, God, as a God of creation, is also a God of justice and a God of the common good because a distributive justice that is not a prerequisite for a common good is not distributive justice.

There is no need to quote more principles. These three principles⁵⁵ are essential to the promotion of the common good in Congo. By respecting them, the Congolese authorities would already take a major step towards development; and this for the happiness of all Congolese.

This chapter focused on promoting social and economic justice for the Congo. I started with the idea that politics cannot ignore ethics. This observation has been made considering the large gap that exists between politics and ethics in Africa, especially in Congo; a contradiction which suggests that ethics is expressly

50. Hollenbach, *Common Good*, 193.
51. Quoted by Hollenbach, *Common Good*, 193.
52. Hollenbach, *Common Good*, 195.
53. Hollenbach, "Common Good in a Divided Society," 1.
54. Hollenbach, "Common Good in a Divided Society," 1.
55. Namely, the respect of the human person, the ethical norms for economic life, and the moral priorities for the nation.

overlooked in politics. If this were not the case, why neglect to promote the well-being of all, if indeed the human person is central to the African ethics? To answer this question, I elected to start with Bujo, an African ethicist who through his book highlights some aspects of the African ethics. I showed that in applying the ethics of Africa, the Congo would have no problem with social and economic justice, since African ethics gives a privileged place to the good of the community. I concluded that, in Congo, the good of the community is neglected in favor of a few individuals. This led me to think that the problem of the common good is first and foremost a political problem. In other words, because the African ethics is expressly forgotten the Congolese do not benefit from oil revenues. Then, I sought to identify the cause of this failure; first through the Congolese Constitution, then through the understanding that the Congolese politicians have of the common good.

In a second section, I call upon authors who address the concept of common good in a perspective that would be attractive to the Congo. Sacks's understanding seemed eloquent as he presents society as a home we build together. Maritain and Thomas Aquinas have provided an understanding of the common good based on the human person. Finally, I turned to the American bishops, who through their pastoral letter made a clear presentation of the concept of economic and social justice. Three principles of their letter stand out in my mind as being especially important: moral priorities, ethical norms, and human dignity.

These principles, like those raised by Bujo, Sacks, Maritain, and Thomas Aquinas, can help the Congolese church to build a solid strategy for social and economic justice worthy of the Congo.

This brings us to the next and final chapter.

FOUR

Strategy of Action

THE EMERGENCE OF ECONOMIC and social justice in the Republic of Congo cannot be achieved without a strategy for action. This must take account of the anthropological perspective presented by Mveng in his theory of anthropological pauperization. A recourse to the African Christological perspective is also necessary. In this context, Nyamiti is a great help. It would also be important to have recourse to Congolese literature by following, for example, Dongala. At the same time, the social analytic perspective cannot prevent us from examining the Congolese ethos without recourse to the Catholic Social Teaching, theology, philosophy, etc. Indeed, an ethical solution to the Congolese problem requires a paradigm that must consider such essential notions as transparency and good governance, the promotion of peace, attention to who benefits from oil profits, the imperative of listening to the people, respect for the written law, etc. The social analysis proposed in this chapter is inspired by Wariboko.

Various concerns need to be taken into consideration by the Congolese Catholic Church regarding the promotion of social and

The Role of the Congolese Catholic Church

economic justice in relation to oil. If the Church wants to succeed, she must build a strategy of action. It is only in doing so that she can be the "voice of the voiceless" and therefore continue her advocacy, necessary to the flourishing of the Congolese society. Such advocacy is a prerequisite for the advent of a new, better, just, democratic, and flourishing Congo.

This chapter proceeds as follows: first it provides some considerations relevant to an effective and realistic analysis of the Congolese situation. Concretely, I present the problem in Mveng's language. Further, I will also add several other perspectives: theological (including Christological), literary, and social analytic. The first examination is through anthropology.

From an Anthropological Perspective

To begin with, let us acknowledge, following Engelbert Mveng,[1] that the starting-point of the Negro-African thought is not the being as being, but the most fundamental human experience, the experience of life and of the living man. In other words, the Negro-African thought deals with anthropology and not ontology as does Western thought.[2] It is important to mention this because in this reflection what is at stake is Congolese man's life. Corruption and embezzlement endanger the life of most of the Congolese people. This endangers the future of the Congolese society as well as the

---

1. Mveng, a Jesuit from Cameroon, was an historian, a theologian, a painter, as well as a poet. Well known in the African continent as well as abroad for his works in anthropology, history, art, etc., he was murdered in April 1995 in Yaoundé (Cameroon). Moreover, Mveng is known for his theory of "*paupérisation anthropologique*" (translated as "anthropological pauperization") that he uses to explain why Africa is poor.

2. This argument is sustained by Mveng, *Afrique dans l'Église*, 10. Indeed, it is relevant to know that the Negro-African thought is based on anthropology instead of ontology. Congo being an African country, it is easier to focus on anthropology to better understand the situation in this country. In other words, it doesn't make any sense to follow the ontological view because Congo is not a Western country. See also Kibangou, *Mvengian Vision of Anthropological Pauperization*, 26–36. On the same topic read Bujo, *Foundations of an African Ethic*, 20–51.

future of the whole country. The World Bank states for example that, among the many characteristics of the Congolese sociopolitical context which caused tensions and fueled civil war, the following have been the most important: (i) mismanagement of the country's rich natural resources (in particular, oil); (ii) pervasive poverty and unequal distribution of income; (iii) exclusion of youth; (iv) opportunistic exploitation of ethnicity; and (v) an unstable sub-regional context.[3]

These words by the World Bank express the gravity of the situation in Congo. This gravity is also affirmed by the Congolese bishops who state that "our oil must be an instrument for the life and not the death of our people."[4] This shows how Mveng is correct in saying that the Negro African thought is anthropological and not ontological because what is at stake is human life or human rights.

In fact, what I wrote above about corruption and embezzlement endangering the future of the Congolese society must be considered first in its anthropological consequences, namely, pauperizarion. It is not only poverty because of human wrongdoing, but also pauperization as a threat to the Congolese society. It is paradoxically the worsening of poverty in a context of oil production. I use the word *paradoxical* because there is an anthropological argument that "democratization and transparency in the management of oil revenues, (is) crucial to lift African people in resource-rich countries out of poverty."[5] In other words, if the management of oil revenues does not help the Congo to get out of poverty, it means that there is a problem of democratization or transparency. This is for example the point of view of Bishop Louis Portella Mbuyu who "has vocally engaged with the Congolese government, as well as European extractive companies, on the issues of democratization and of transparency in the management of oil revenues, for the economic and social benefit of the population."[6]

3. World Bank, *Transitional Support Strategy*, i.
4. Quoted by McDonald and Gary, "Integrated Approaches," 88.
5. Agenzia Fides, "Delegation of African Bishops," 1.
6. Agenzia Fides, "Delegation of African Bishops," 1.

The Role of the Congolese Catholic Church

This perspective of explaining poverty by means of mismanagement of oil revenues is plausible and convenient in the Congolese situation. However, there is another reason for explaining poverty in Africa as well as in the Congo.

According to Mveng, the context of Africa is a context of poverty, misery, and impoverishment or pauperization.[7] In fact, Mveng has described better than anyone else the many perspectives of the African context. For him, the way people suffer in Africa, including in the Congo, is better illustrated by the notion of "anthropological pauperization."

The construct of anthropological pauperization largely explains that people are not poor, but they are made poor. Indeed, following Mveng, the Congolese people are made poor by their own government with the complicity of other actors such as oil companies. That is why Mveng states, "Our context today is a new experience of enslavement and domination by the powers controlling the world."[8] What Mveng says about Africa remains true in the Congolese society, for what happens is that those who have power enslave the Congolese people and try to maintain their control over the Congo. From this perspective one can understand poverty in Africa as well as in the Congo.

In addition, the expression "powers controlling the world" can be used in the Congolese situation. Indeed, oil companies control the Congo, beginning with the former French company Elf, now TotalFinaElf.[9] For example, what Loïk Le Floch-Prigent says is very evocative:

> Elf is not only an oil company. It is a parallel diplomacy destined to keep control over a certain number of African states, most of all at the key moment of decolonization. Elf was created to function as an oil company, and that worked perfectly, but it also acts as an extension of

---

7. These terms refer to the dialectical character of poverty. One is not merely poor, one is made poor.

8. Mveng, "Impoverishment and Liberation," 154. See also Freire, *Pedagogy of the Oppressed*, 50–80.

9. Koula, *Pétrole et violences au Congo-Brazzaville*, 50–60.

the state, so that African politics conforms nicely with the state's interests.[10]

These words are shocking for a company that is supposed to do only business. Indeed, this poses an ethical as well as political problem. It is an ethical problem because it deals with bad behavior on the part of an oil company that does more than it should. But it is also a political problem because it concerns the sovereignty of a state, namely, the Republic of Congo.

However, I will not overemphasize this point because it is not the subject of this reflection, although it is connected to oil. I mention this problem to emphasize an aspect no less important to the management of oil in the Congo.

Another aspect that explains the worsening poverty in the Congo is the following: people who belong to the family of the president have no problem with money; they have everything they ask for.[11] Children of the current president do whatever they want. The same happens with those who helped the president to come to power by a coup d'état.[12] Indeed, these people spend millions of dollars with no accounting to the public treasury.

This applies to all political regimes that succeed another, even though with the current regime, financial scandals have multiplied because of the oil boom and the rising price of a barrel of oil.

All things considered; we can say that poverty in the Congo is a "political problem"[13] because it is largely aggravated by the behavior of politicians. Such bad behavior is a defect that strikes or threatens individuals, families, or a certain social class in the

10. Knight, *Brazzaville Charms*, 129.

11. For more information see Dulin and Merckaert, *Bien mal acquis*, 8.

12. They call it their contribution to "*l'effort de guerre*" (translated as "the war effort"). In other words, they have everything they want because of their contribution to the war of 1997 that brought the current president to power.

13. I quote this from Mveng, who thinks that "poverty as we experience it today in Africa is indeed a political problem. However, the problem is not identical in Africa and in the West. European approaches present poverty as an internal political problem of the societies and states concerned. . . . Alas, none of this is applicable in today's Africa, either to the citizen or to the state" (Mveng, "Impoverishment and Liberation", 156).

Congo. This is unfortunately the case in many African countries as it appears in the theory of anthropological pauperization by Mveng.

According to Mveng, in Africa as well as in the Congo poverty strikes the state first.[14] Mentioning this, I do not digress from the topic. Instead, I bring an additional explanation for the understanding of poverty in the Congo. In other words, those who are in power lead a poor state[15] (but one rich in natural resources), by pauperizing the people by means of corruption and embezzlement.

In addition, following Mveng, poverty is also multidimensional. It has different faces: moral, cultural, sociological, etc. In fact, these types of poverty are not separable in Africa or in the Congo (likewise in the Third World) from material poverty.

Material poverty produces misery that is defined as "the state of absolute indigence in which a human being, deprived of everything, lives in conditions at times inferior to those of an animal."[16] As we see it, poverty in Africa, including in the Congo is, according to Mveng, anthropological and structural. By anthropological, Mveng means material poverty as well as moral, intellectual, and sociological poverty.

Anthropological Pauperization

In the Republic of Congo, poverty is anthropological when the Congolese people cannot benefit from oil revenues. They are

---

14. We can see that Mveng sees material poverty as the fundamental poverty. Some researchers propose two different ways of defining poverty: absolute poverty and relative poverty. Absolute poverty refers to the situation in which a person lacks those things that help to sustain human life (basic needs like food, clothing and shelter). This poverty is common to many Third World countries. Relative poverty refers to the situation in which a person lacks the necessary resources to participate in the normal and desirable patterns of life. In a certain way, material poverty can be understood as fundamental poverty as Marxists do.

15. Congo is also a country impoverished by debt. I will explain further how and why.

16. Mveng, "Impoverishment and Liberation", 154–56.

Strategy of Action

anthropologically poor for lack of goods, possessions, identity, freedom, rights, and hope for the future, etc. As Mveng puts it:

> When persons are deprived not only of goods and possessions of a material, spiritual, moral, intellectual, cultural, or sociological order, but of everything that makes up the foundation of their-being-in-the-world and the specificity of their "ipseity" as individual, society, and history.... It is this poverty that we call anthropological poverty. This is an indigence of being, the legacy of centuries of slavery and colonization. It has long since banished us Africans from world history and the world map.[17]

When Mveng talks about anthropological poverty, it is important to mention that it has many levels: pseudo-philanthropic, corruptive, debt, and cultural. To avoid digressing, I insist only on two levels: corruptive and debt, about oil.

Pauperization is also debt. It is, according to Mveng, the most oppressive because it is based on a system of reduction of slavery of peoples and countries, condemned for life to work for an unknown master. Here Mveng has in mind debts that African people, including Congolese, did not contract.[18] Indeed, Mveng is right in mentioning the problem of debt.

There is a big gap between these two words: *debt* and *contract*. In fact, how can one understand that Congo, an oil-producing country, is one of the most indebted countries in the world,[19] when more than 70 percent of the Congolese people live on less than a dollar per day? In the Congolese situation it is important to point out that such a debt is odious.

---

17. Mveng, "Impoverishment and Liberation," 156.

18. This concept reminds us of another one: "dette odieuse" (translated as "odious debt"). For more details, see Ndikumana and Boyce, *Dette odieuse de l'Afrique*; International Monetary Fund, "IMF and Word Bank Announce," 1–3.

19. Per capita.

According to Jeff King, Ashfaq Khalfan, and Bryan Thomas,[20] there are three conditions which make a debt odious. First, there is no consent because the debt was incurred without the consent of the people. Second, there is no benefit for funds were spent contrary to the interests of the population. Finally, there is knowledge of the interests of the borrower by the creditor. All these conditions summarize what an odious debt is. The economic situation of the Congo is a good example of odious debt. Poverty is also structural because it threatens individuals as well as communities or the state.

Structural Pauperization

Besides being anthropological, poverty in Africa, thus in the Congo, is also structural; it deals with the state. According to Mveng, structural impoverishment or structural poverty is the essence of the structure because it threatens the institutions of African countries due to the historical circumstances of the advent of independence. As Mveng puts it:

> Our poverty is not only many-sided (at once material, spiritual, moral, intellectual, cultural, sociological, and so on); it is above all else anthropological and structural. . . . If we accept the word impoverishment (pauperization) as denoting either the fact of one's becoming poor (passive meaning), or the act of making someone poor (active meaning), we are obliged to observe that the phenomenon of impoverishment, in black Africa today, is comprehensive, total, and absolute, on the continent, in the states, in the cities as in the countryside.[21]

As described, such poverty puts everyone and everything in question because life becomes a real struggle for individuals, social groups, and even entire nations.

---

20. Jeff King, Ashfaq Khalfan, and Bryan Thomas are Canadian scholars. Khalfan et al., "Advancing the Odious Debt Doctrine," 2–3.

21. Mveng, "Impoverishment and Liberation," 156.

In the case of the Congo, it is almost shocking. If the country is oil-producing, oil revenues should help the country to move forward. But revenues are used wrongly, and the Congolese people cannot benefit from them. If our politicians were aware of this dual situation (anthropological poverty and structural poverty), and less selfish, they would recognize the poverty of the Congolese people and make efforts to eradicate it. Unfortunately, their behavior makes the situation worse and creates new poor.

Nevertheless, these two types of extreme poverty and the behavior of the Congolese politicians do not explain the whole Congolese situation. There are often mechanisms such as malice, violence, structures of sins, ethnic confrontations, and so forth that require deeper analysis. From an anthropological perspective let us move on to an African Christological or theological perspective.

From an African Christological Perspective

A social-scientific examination of the mismanagement of oil in the Congolese society can be explained christologically. Christology must be understood in its theological dimension.

This section focuses on Christian African Christology. Indeed, two approaches are present in African Christology, namely, inculturation[22] and liberation. In the words of Charles Nyamiti, "Inculturation involves an effort to incarnate Christian teaching in African cultures on the level of theology or Christology." There are basically two different ways of doing Christology in Africa. For example, Christology can be done following African traditions, or following Christian African Christologies. According to Charles Nyamiti, "various forms of African Christologies correspond to different kinds of African theology: the 'non-christian' (traditional) and Christian African Christologies, comprise the

---

22. For more information see Bujo, *African Christian Morality*; Ikechukwu Odozor, "African Moral Theology," 583–609.

The Role of the Congolese Catholic Church

nonscientific and scientific types."[23] Therefore, an analysis of the Congolese ethos cannot ignore Nyamiti's words.

As I said in a previous chapter, in addition to the Catholic Church, there are other churches in the Congo such as Kimbanguist, Protestant, Orthodox, and the like. Even though these other churches play a significant role in the Congolese society, the purpose of this reflection is not to address them but to focus on the Catholic Church.

About Christology in Africa, and following Nyamiti, two approaches are possible. The first approach suggests a symbiosis between African cultures and the Christian teaching. This constitutes an inculturation approach, as it were. The second approach is liberation, which deals with South African Black theology "centered on racial or color factor (apartheid)" and the African liberation theology "found especially in the independent part of Africa, which has a broader perspective than that of South Africa."[24]

If I had to choose between the two approaches, regarding the Congolese situation, I would obviously choose the African liberation theology because the Congolese people need theologians who can help them to overcome poverty, corruption, embezzlement, and the like.

Amid many aspects presented in the liberation approach, the aspect of ministry seems to be the most indicated. Here Engelbert Mveng again emerges. For him the gospel does not beatify poverty. What the gospel does is to show the way of liberation and salvation of the poor. The poor in African ministry are seen with the dignity of daughters and sons of God. That is why Mveng considers that poverty and its mechanisms are anti-evangelical.

Unfortunately, in the Congo, oil is the cause of such anti-values as inequity, injustice, poverty, and the like. Aware of this, the Congolese bishops stated, "A number of ills plaguing our country result from the mismanagement of oil revenues [. . . that] leads to inequality, injustice, war and poverty, leisure mentality, a source of

---

23. Nyamiti, "Contemporary African Christologies," 63–67.
24. Nyamiti, "Contemporary African Christologies," 65–66.

neglect of vital sectors of the economy, public debt."[25] These words show the seriousness of the situation in the Congo; they cannot leave indifferent the Congolese politicians, because it is their fault that the country is in this situation. Indeed, even though these words by the bishops date back to 2002, they portray the state in which the Congo found itself in 2002, i.e., just a few years after the war brought about by the oil. It is also in this context that we understand Anatole Milandou, then archbishop of Brazzaville, who declared during war: "Oil has become one of the main challenges of fighting. Production is important, but the people never heard of oil or barrels or dollars: he only knows the number of deaths. Nowadays, they plunder, they bombard, and they kill for oil."[26] While this observation is bitter, it shows a reality that we all know: Oil is a source of violence in many African countries. Unfortunately, the Congo is no exception to this observation.

In this regard, the article "Oil, Arms and Violence in Africa" by Daniel Volman is evocative. In this article, the author offers an analysis of oil-producing countries that have not been spared by the war. The report is frightening: "The possession of oil resources, and the revenues that accrue to governments from the exploitation of this resource, have had a decisive impact on the security and stability of nearly every African country that has significant amounts of oil."[27] The list of countries concerned is impressive: Angola, Sudan, Nigeria,[28] Chad, and finally the Republic of Congo. It includes more than 333,358,923[29] people. Angola: 36,684,202; Sudan: 48,109,006; Nigeria: 223,804,632; Chad: 18,618, 903; and finally the Congo: 6,142,180.[30]

In the Congolese situation, poverty appears as the main social problem that threatens the Congolese citizens. Somehow,

---

25. Billets d'Afrique, "Ingérences épiscopales."
26. Billets d'Afrique, "Ingérences épiscopales," 5.
27. Volman, "Oil, Arms, and Violence," 1.
28. Okowa, *Political Economy of Development Planning in Nigeria*, 55–80; Okowa, *Oil, Systemic Corruption, Abdulistic Capitalism*, 30–55.
29. Population Today, "Population d'Afrique 2024," 1.
30. Institut National de la Statistique, *Résultats préliminaires*, viii.

poverty is considered as misery. The problem of misery might be seen as a challenge for ministry because the Lord came to deliver us from misery.

> That is what Zechariah sings at the beginning of St. Luke's Gospel (Luke 1:68–79), that is what the Magnificat proclaims (Luke 1:47–55), that is what the charter of the Beatitudes promulgates (Matt. 5:1–12), and that is what the Lord himself reveals in the synagogue at Nazareth, as he inaugurates his public ministry (Luke 4:18–20).[31]

Those who want to discover resources to help the Congolese people fight poverty must have in mind the image of Jesus as liberator.[32] Indeed, the 70 percent of the Congolese people who live poorly need liberation by means of theology.

From African Christology, it is also relevant to see if people in power have religious values. In the Republic of Congo, some claim to be Christians. If they are really Christians, this might be a serious problem for the Catholic Church. How to advocate good governance when those who govern us are Christians? I trust that this is not the case.

The fact remains that most politicians in power are Freemasons,[33] beginning with the president. In this situation what policy and what attitude should be taken? In other words, a Christological assessment will consider all these data. What does Congolese literature have to say on this point?

From Congolese Literature

From a literary point of view, the novel *Johnny Mad Dog* by the Congolese author Emmanuel Dongala is very evocative about the

---

31. Mveng, "Impoverishment and Liberation," 163.

32. Sobrino, *Jesus the Liberator*, 53–55; Sobrino, *Christ the Liberator*, 39–40. The reason I evoke Sobrino is that the context of Latin America and Africa are similar, even though the way in which the Latin American context is presented is quite different from the African one.

33. This is known to most Congolese because there are videos on YouTube, for example.

Strategy of Action

war that the Congo experienced in 1997. The movie of the same name, directed by Jean-Stéphane Sauvaire, is based on this novel. Even if the context of the movie was Liberia, it analyzes what happened in the Congo during the fueled war. The following comment says it all:

> Congo, right now. Johnny, sixteen years old, dressed in his fatigues and his T-shirt encrusted with broken glass, armed to the teeth, inhabited by the bad dog he wants to become, steals, rapes, pillages and kills everything that crosses his path. Laokolé, sixteen years old, pushing his mother with broken legs in a rickety wheelbarrow, trying to invent the radiant future that his brilliant schooling promised him, tries to flee his town delivered to the militias of child soldiers. Under the windows of embassies, NGOs, the High Commissioner for Refugees, and under the eyes of Western television, teenagers soaked in Hollywood imagery and disguised information play war: militias fight enemies called "Chechens," the warlords, who stick very closely to their codes of honor, call themselves "Rambo" or "Giap" and kill each other over a radio, a basket of fruit or a crooked word.[34]

The reason I chose this novel as an example is that it recounts a war in a country whose oil was the main cause of that war. As in many African countries that have experienced war, victims are often children, women, and the old men and women.

Indeed, in 1997, after the civil war of 1993–94, the Congo experienced another civil war between militias controlled by three political figures: the then-president Pascal Lissouba, the former (and current) president Denis Sassou-Nguesso, and the former prime minister Bernard Kolelas. As Anne Sundberg states:

> The Congo's natural resources have always been the object of a power struggle rather than the basis for development and improvement of living conditions for its people. . . . The emerging picture shows an ongoing disintegration of policy and society. The disintegrative tendencies take

---

34. Dongala, *Johnny Mad Dog*, cover. See also de Beer and Cornwell, "Congo-Brazzaville," 1–7.

> the form of feudalization in the sense that various feudal lords use their own groups and militias to gain access to the throne. This kind of disintegration has recently accelerated. The state no longer constitutes a supreme authority with a monopoly over the use of force. Instead a number of feudal lords/warlords claim an equal right to supremacy and to their own territories. In the present conflict ex-President Sassou N'Guesso demanded that President Lissouba himself should sign the peace treaty, which the latter refused to do, arguing that Sassou was not his equal and that the Prime Minister, at a lower level in the hierarchy, would be the right person to do it. In today's Congo each feudal lord has his own militia to protect his territory. One of them even administers his own port and the collection of customs dues in Brazzaville.[35]

Although much has changed from 1997 to 2011, these words of Anne Sundberg are very revealing of the period of war in the Congo, and of its consequences. This brings us to a social analysis perspective.

From a Social Analysis Perspective

A social-scientific examination of the problem that threatens the Congolese society, namely corruption and embezzlement, can be done from a philosophical ethics view. The construct of philosophy is understood as a study of the fundamental principles of an activity, praxis, and a reflection on their meaning and legitimacy. Relating to the Congolese society, one of the philosophical domains that makes this analysis possible is ethics. Indeed, ethics deals with our actions and behaviors, at both individual and communal levels.

With this end in view, one understands why, by putting in relation different categories,[36] it is possible to have a wide picture

---

35. Sundberg, "Class and Ethnicity," 2–3. See also Lumumba-Kasongo, "Congo-Brazzaville," 12–15; Zartman and Vogeli, "Prevention Gained and Prevention Lost," 265–92. For more details read Eaton, "Diagnosing the Crisis," 44–46; Tonda, "Guerre dans le 'camp Nord,'" 50–67.

36. "Fragility," "egoism," "death of the multitude," "life of a minority,"

of the moral problem that the Congolese people face and come to understand the relationship between those categories and the Congolese society.

In the following section I will undertake a "critical and constructive investigation" of the social problem that threatens the Congolese society. Having said this, four conditions are relevant: an ultimate concern that serves as a *telos* of the Congolese society; obstacles and resistance to the realization of the "ought to be"; a desire to overcome such resistance; and finally, the will to oppose proffered solutions.

Examination of the Congolese Ethos

The purpose of this section is to look at the Congolese ethos and point out how it relates to the problem of mismanagement, poverty, and embezzlement. Concretely, it is a task of identifying a web of values and norms, and organizing principles of the Congolese society about the problem that threatens the present and the future of the Congolese people.

The main argument of this section is that there is, in the Congolese imaginary, an interpretation of the war that the Congo experienced in 1997. This interpretation is simply a product of the colonial process of production of ethnicity in sub-Saharan Africa. This colonial process divided the country into two blocks: the South and the North; a North bangala or mbochi on the one hand, and a South kongo on the other hand.[37] Therefore, the 1997 war can be interpreted in the North-South divide.[38] In other words, it is an update of the founding myth of political

---

"crucifixion of the people," "emotions," "evil," "pain," "suffering," "corruption," "injustice," "compassion," "crime," "good," "search for justice," "embezzlement," "mismanagement," "theft," "poverty," "wealth," "struggle," and "unhappiness."

37. Tonda, "Guerre dans le 'camp Nord,'" 50; Clark, "Resource Revenues and Political Development," 25–26.

38. This interpretation is wrong because the 1993–94 civil war pitted supporters of Lissouba against supporters of Kolelas, and both are from the South.

violence[39] in the Congo: the 1959 war pitted "Mbochi" of Jacques Opangault against "Lari" of Abbot Fulbert Youlou.[40]

Indeed, if the ethnic argument does not pass, the rest must be found elsewhere. In the words of Joseph Tonda, the North-South war in 1997 was an illusion, based on an ideology. This ideology concealed two realities inextricably linked: violent expression of the relationship between factions of the political class around the conquest or the preservation of state power, on the one hand; and the material issue around which oppositions are structured, and violence's class are based.[41] This interpretation by Joseph Tonda is plausible and somehow justifies the war for control of oil. There are several reasons to be given based on the history and the symbolic system. The story is that of class relations and the symbolic system refers to beliefs, mythical narratives, rituals, and fantasy.[42]

Indeed, in the words of Joseph Tonda, stories of class conflicts are structured around socioeconomic issues. And the Congolese case can be told in an imaginary language to produce a scientific narrative. The first scientific narrative is that there was a self-fulfilling prophecy: the 1997 war in the Congo was prescribed, expected.[43] Concretely, the war began on June 5, 1997, and ended on October 15, 1997. During that war General Sassou Nguesso was anxious not to ratify the thesis of a coup d'état.[44] Different ideas explain this.

The first is the opposition between North and South. We said that this idea does not pass the test of adequacy, because of the 1993 war that pitted southerners against each other. The second is an extension of the first: a declination on the mode of a revealed

---

39. Obenga, *Histoire sanglante du Congo-Brazzaville*, 26–98; Makouta-Mboukou, *Destruction de Brazzaville*, 19–99. See also Gauze, *The Politics of Congo-Brazzaville*.

40. Tonda, "Guerre dans le 'camp Nord,'" 51.

41. Tonda, "Guerre dans le 'camp Nord,'" 52.

42. Tonda, "Guerre dans le 'camp Nord,'" 52.

43. Tonda, "Guerre dans le 'camp Nord,'" 53.

44. According to Joseph Tonda, Sassou's idea was of maintaining the war until August 31. This was the end date of the mandate of Lissouba. For more information read de Beer and Cornwell, "Congo-Brazzaville."

truth, the discourse of ethnicity.[45] The logic of this declination would argue that all northerners are behind Sassou, an idea based on ethnicity, while the real problem was the control of power and thus consequently a grip on oil. Third, it treats a president in power as if he were a foreigner. Lissouba was thus referred to as a pygmy. The pygmies are considered aliens, non-human. In the words of Joseph Tonda, all Congolese presidents encountered the same experience as Lissouba did, namely, treated as if they were foreigners to their ethnic communities. This is very present in the Congolese imaginary.

All these examples are indicative of the subconscious of the Congolese politicians. They are willing to do anything to gain power. For them ethnicity is a fundamental issue of war. But for them what is most important is the relationship of men to things. As Joseph Tonda puts it, "the relationship of men to things is simultaneously a relationship between men, power and state."[46] These words require no commentary. They say a great deal about how oil can be managed by politicians.

In the mindset of these politicians there is allowed the plundering of natural resources or property of any kind, theft, corruption, and embezzlement. Indeed, for these men, there is a difference between looting and stealing. As Joseph Tonda puts it, "pillage ezali pillage, ezali moyibi te."[47]

Another expression more directly linked to oil is as follows: "pillage ezali Nkossa, chacun aura sa part."[48] This expression is also a mixture of Lingala and French. It means "looting is Nkossa,[49] everyone will have a part." This expression is attributed to former president Lissouba when the oil deposits of Nkossa were discovered. He promised that everyone would share in the oil money.

---

45. Tonda, "Guerre dans le 'camp Nord,'" 54.
46. Tonda, "Guerre dans le 'camp Nord,'" 59.
47. Tonda, "Guerre dans le 'camp Nord,'" 61. This is a mixture of Lingala (one of the Congolese national language besides Kikongo) and French, which means "looting is not stealing."
48. Tonda, "Guerre dans le 'camp Nord,'" 61.
49. Nkossa is an oil field off Pointe-Noire.

The Role of the Congolese Catholic Church

Some people misinterpret this as saying that everyone would have his or her part of war, because instead of receiving money, they received a war brought on by oil.

It is worth pointing out that oil is seen by many Congolese as the cause of their misfortune. Indeed, they think that oil has divided them into social classes. On one hand we have the rich and on the other the poor. The rich are those who profit from the country's wealth. As the saying goes, a goat grazes where it is tied.[50] In other words, when a person is promoted to a political post, those in his entourage are promoted. This is a caricature but says much about the behavior of the Congolese politicians regarding money or what money symbolizes, namely oil.

Indeed, access to oil highlights another aspect of social relations: consumption/consummation in social representations.[51] It is this consumption/consummation which is presented in the Congolese imaginary by the following expressions: "*kaka feti na feti*,"[52] or "*ledza, lenua, leyiba*."[53]

The above description does not mean that the entire Congolese society is implicated in such approaches. It does not involve all social strata. That is why the agents of the civil society want to change things. Among them is the Catholic Church. Indeed, "the Congolese people need to participate, fully and freely, in the running of their country. The Church as well as the rest of the civil society has the responsibility to work towards the emergence of such a society."[54] These words by Séraphin Ngouma show us that the Congolese people do not want their country to forfeit values like work, integrity, etc. That is why they rely on the Church and the rest of civil society to help bring about a worthy and just society. This brings us to the next step in our analysis.

50. This is an interpretation that allows looting, and therefore corruption.
51. Tonda, "Guerre dans le 'camp Nord,'" 64.
52. In Lingala language, this means "a permanent celebration."
53. In Mbochi language this means "eat, drink, steal."
54. Ngouma, "Responsibility of the Church," 12.

STRATEGY OF ACTION

Resources for Reflecting on the Problem

This section focuses on resources needed to reflect upon the problem of the Congolese society. Theological, philosophical, and biblical resources will assist those who seek to address what threatens the Congolese people.

Two steps are important in this section. The first step deals with the "resources that will be brought to inform and shape the discourse of the problem."[55] In other words, what is important here is to say which theology or approach is necessary for addressing the problem. The second step is about "analyzing the operating norms in the ethos to see if they are basically right."[56]

The Resources to Shape the Discourse

I basically rely on three types of speech or resources: biblical, theological, and philosophical or ethical. I will touch on each succinctly, focusing on a few highlights.

BIBLICAL RESOURCE

By biblical I mean a reference to the Scriptures, as well as to the biblical bases of Catholic Social Teaching (CST).

I selected a verse that I think is important: "*The good person brings good things out of a good treasure, and the evil person brings evil things out of an evil treasure.*"[57]

My interpretation of this verse is based on the management of oil by politicians. Because of its misuse, oil appears to be a dangerous thing in the eyes of the Congolese people. In this sense, oil appears as a treasure that rhymes with death in the Congolese imagination. Many families were torn apart because of the successive wars over oil.

---

55. Wariboko, "Ethical Methodology," 13.
56. Wariboko, "Ethical Methodology," 13.
57. Matt 12:35.

From a biblical perspective, we can therefore say that politicians must try to make oil a treasure that brings good news, not death to the Congolese. Indeed, in applying this verse from Matthew, it would seem to indict the Congolese politicians. Therefore, it is a challenge for them to change their behavior.

On the other hand, CST teaches us through the voice of Pope John Paul II that:

> This teaching comes into being ... from the presence of Christians in the midst of the world's changing situations and their contact with the resultant challenges. So this social doctrine entails not only principles for reflection, but also norms for judgment and guidelines for action.[58]

These words by John Paul II are relevant in the Congolese case; they contain clues that can be useful for the management of oil. Following Peter Henriot, SJ, these indices can be summarized in three principles, norms and guidelines:

- To guide individual consciences in making just decisions
- To shape the response of the church to social issues
- To influence the activities of the public sector.[59]

Indeed, these principles recall others, namely the methodology of look, judge, and act. These words were spoken by Pope John XXIII in his encyclical letter *Mater et Magistra*:

> There are three stages which should normally be followed in the reduction of social principles into practice. First, one reviews the concrete situation; secondly, one forms a judgment on it in the light of these same principles; thirdly, one decides what in the circumstances can and should be done to implement these principles. These

---

58. Quoted in McDonald, *Transparency*, 5; Warner and Alexander, "Enhancing Economic Performance," 5–6.

59. McDonald, *Transparency*, 5. See also Giroux, "Africa's Growing Strategic Relevance," 1–3.

are the three stages usually expressed in the three terms: look, judge, act.[60]

There are several things to point out when making use of these three principles for the management of oil in the Congo. First, "instead of bringing prosperity, the oil boom has been accompanied by years of violent conflict and war, often fought over oil rents; 70% of the population lives below the poverty line."[61] This principle refers to the first principle: look. Secondly, "up until the Church had spoken out, it was taboo to even talk about what was happening to oil revenue . . . . The climate of fear had now been reduced slightly, spaces for dialogue were beginning to open, and people felt more able to discuss these issues in public."[62] These words of Bishop Louis Portella Mbuyu show how important it was for people to speak courageously of problems that plague the country, beginning with oil. They did so because they found it appropriate to do so. In other words, they found it appropriate to make judgments. The third and final principle is encapsulated in the campaign "PWYP"[63] (Publish What You Pay), a call to action. This brings us to the theological resource.

Theological Resource

The theological discourse is based on documents such as *Gaudium et Spes*, in which it is said:

---

60. John XXIII, *Mater et Magistra*, no. 236; Wariboko, "Ethical Methodology," 13.

61. McDonald, *Transparency*, 10.

62. Portella Mbuyu, quoted by McDonald, *Transparency*, 11.

63. According to McDonald, "the PWYP Coalition now consists of over one hundred and thirty nongovernmental organizations (NGOs) from throughout the world. The coalition argues that companies should be transparent about revenue payments made to governments so that civil society can accurately assess whether money is being misappropriated, lobby for full transparency in local government spending and hold their governments to account" (*Transparency*, 7). See also Afeikhena et al., "Addressing Oil Related Corruption," 21–32.

God has destined the earth and all it contains for the use of everyone and of all peoples, so that the good things of creation should be available equally to all ... For this reason, in making use of them, we ought to regard the exterior things we lawfully possess not just as our own but also as common, in the sense that they can profit not only the owners but other also.[64]

These are words of extraordinary eloquence. They promote the concept of the common good and indicate the origin of all things: God.

In the book *Living Justice: Catholic Social Teaching in Action*, Thomas Massaro, SJ, gives a useful list of points that summarize relevant principles of the Catholic Social Teaching such as the dignity of every person and human rights, "solidarity, common good, and participation," "family life, subsidiarity and the proper role of government," "peace and disarmament, option for the poor and vulnerable."[65]

About the issue of oil in Congo, three points deserve our attention. The first is human rights. Massaro states for example that "one important aspect of human dignity is the notion of equality. The Catholic tradition interprets the key moments of the drama of human life in a way that treats all people equally."[66] In a sense, a real promotion of social and economic justice in Congo must consider all the Congolese people equally. If I insist on this point, it is because the lives of many Congolese people are not taken into consideration by the state. Many Congolese live "naked," as it were. This expression calls to mind the words of Giorgio Agamben: "form-of-life" that is "a life that can never be separated from its form, a life in which it is never possible to isolate something such as naked life."[67] According to Agamben "a life that cannot be separated from its form is a life for which what is at stake in its

---

64. *Gaudium et Spes*, no. 69.
65. Massaro, *Living Justice*, 5.
66. Massaro, *Living Justice*, 116.
67. Agamben, *Means without End*, 2–3. See also Agamben, *État d'exception*, 1.

Strategy of Action

way of living is living itself."[68] This is what most of the Congolese people experience in daily life. For them, living is already a problem because "human beings—as beings of power who can do or not do, succeed or fail, lose themselves or find themselves—are the only beings for whom happiness is always at stake in their living."[69] Thus, their lives will change, as Massaro puts it, if they are treated equally.

The second point that deserves our attention is solidarity, common good, and participation. According to Massaro, solidarity "calls attention to the simple and easily observable fact that people are interdependent; they rely upon each other for almost all their biological and social needs."[70] This point seems absent in the case of the Congolese because most of them do not feel interdependent with those who are not poor. In other words, interdependence is absent and is not considered as a necessary fact or a positive value. In other words, considering interdependence would somehow help to reduce poverty in Congo. Besides, there are the concepts of solidarity and participation. In Massaro's words, "we all have an obligation to promote the common good by making whatever contributions are necessary to improve the lives of others.... Each of us has at once a right and duty to participate in the full range of activities and institutions of social life."[71] Indeed, this is what the church is attempting to do in Congo, but for such an action to be effective it must be shared by most of the Congolese population.

A third useful point in Massaro's book is subsidiarity and the proper role of government. This aspect of the problem is relevant in the Congolese case because it directly involves the assistance of the Congolese government. Subsidiarity "refers to the way the various levels of society should relate to each other about the best outcomes for all people." The Latin root of the word *subsidiarity* means "assistance," and in the case of the Congolese, the 70 percent of those who live below the poverty line should be assisted.

68. Agamben, *Means without End*, 2–3.
69. Agamben, *Means without End*, 2–3.
70. Massaro, *Living Justice*, 120.
71. Massaro, *Living Justice*, 122–23.

That is why the state has a key role to play. As Agamben puts it, "the state is a community instituted for the sake of the living and the well living of men in it."[72] However, we must not wait for the state to do something for us. We have an obligation to take care of the poor and to do our best to overcome poverty wherever we are, including in Congo. This brings us to the philosophical resource.

Philosophical or Ethical Resource

The philosophical resource deals here with what Paul Valadier calls "the data of the moral tradition,"[73] namely, laws, customs, morals. For this French Jesuit, a person who leads his life alone doesn't fully exist. Indeed, we cannot live ignoring the existence of others. That is why it is important not to forget the laws that govern our societies. Valadier thinks that laws can serve as a negative criterion highlighting what is to be avoided. Through customs, he points out that almost everyone learns to assume his humanity, not generally, but according to the society in which he must live. Finally, he attaches great importance to the data of the moral life. For him these data must be assumed, because out of them, consciousness would have no consistency or reality.[74] This brings us to the operating norms.

The Operating Norms in the Ethos

This section deals with operating norms, namely, those rules I mentioned above, which concern the relationship that men in power have with things, including oil. From the study on moral obligation, the problem is to see how these standards are fair, in agreement with the laws of God, and with common sense.

Regarding natural resources, I said above that oil was a source of conflict in the Congo because the politicians were fighting to

---

72. Agamben, *Means without End*, 2–3.
73. Valadier, *Des repères pour agir*, 54.
74. Valadier, *Des repères pour agir*, 58.

have control over it. The evidence is that the bishops came to the same conclusion when they asserted that:

> The control of oil manna is at the center of several battles for power in our region. Oil revenues have served as funding for arms purchases and to support private militias in certain States. We fear that tomorrow, some of our States will go to war against each other over shared oil concessions zones.[75]

This is not a good thing because it gives the impression that violence or conflict is a standard for access to power. The Congolese people do not want such a society.

In addition, this standard is contrary to divine law given the fact that God wanted human beings to manage earthly goods for the good of all. In the case of Congo, it appears that oil is primarily intended for men in power. This is unethical because it creates a division between humans and destroys the human solidarity that can reunite men around the common good.

In the words of the bishops from the Central African region, "solidarity is the recognition of the interconnectedness of personal and institutional activities that make up the social fabric of human existence."[76] This solidarity is yet to be achieved in the Congolese society. In other words, the Congo has a long way to go in this regard. This section brings us to the last step of this analysis.

Ethical Solution (Paradigm) and Payoff

There is a possible ethical solution to the problem that threatens the Congolese society which can be divided into three main parts. The first part will focus on a possible solution in dialogue with some authors. The second part will show whether the solution fits into the Congolese ethos. It will also determine whether a new institution is possible or not. The third part will show how the

---

75. McDonald, *Transparency*, 10.
76. McDonald, *Transparency*, 10.

The Role of the Congolese Catholic Church

solution can be perceived in the Congolese society and the possible payoffs to the Congolese community.

Ethical Solution

To build a social ethic based on the management of the common good should be the result of serious reflection.[77] This demands a profound analysis of the context in which Congolese people live. Such an analysis must be done by people of the civil society (Church, lay people, NGOs) and those who have power in the political realm. If some advancement has been made regarding the possible role for the civil society with the "Publish What You Pay" (PWYP) campaign, it is not entirely sufficient. It is only a beginning.

What I propose here is more a paradigm[78] than a response.[79] This paradigm would include small groups according to their fields to make a social analysis of each field regarding the management of the common good, mainly the natural resources such as oil. It should also include specialists (sociologists, economists, philosophers, social scientists, etc.) as well as non-specialists (peasants or farmers, sages, etc.). It would be essential to discover a group capable of leading this. In the case of Congo-Brazzaville, the Church, because of its role in the Congolese political life, may play such a role. Once the work is done, a document should be drawn up and given to the government. Such a document should:

- insist on the emergence of a real civil society, aware of its mission and aware of the meaning or sense of itself that makes public the mismanagement of the common good.

---

77. Kibangou, "'Diagnostic' de la société congolaise," 7.

78. By this I mean a theoretical model of thought that guides any research or any reflection.

79. By this I mean a solution, explanation, clarification to a question or an obscure point. See Balogun, "Diversity Factors in State Construction Efforts," 65–99.

Strategy of Action

- show the importance and necessity of sharing the common good.

- promote a theory of social and economic justice based on African ethics that promotes the wisdom of palaver. As Anne Sundberg states, "this is, in fact, a traditional strategy, the African palaver and the traditional mode of consensus-seeking. This model may, however, appear more democratic than it really is. It is always power holders who make this model work."[80]

- give the media more and more importance. The Catholic Church already has radio stations (Radio Maria) and could have television stations with programs on the management of natural resources formatted in national languages such as Lingala and Kikongo.

- develop a credible political opposition, an alternative to political power.

- promote an educational system that integrates both a traditional education and modern education. By a traditional system, I refer to the characteristics that Joseph Ki-Zerbo speaks of. "It was an education by and for the community"; "the education was concrete and pragmatic"; "it is a progressive education"; "it is a democratic and an egalitarian education."[81]

- promote freedom of speech and protest without violence. Indeed, people must feel free to protest in a non-violent way.

- emphasize the need for all ethnic groups to live together in harmony for a better Congo.

"Ethnicity may be explosive when it is politicized. Ethnic war and ethnic cleansing took place in 1993, in a situation where different ethnic groups had intermarried and where their children consequently were mixed."[82] Indeed, Congolese politicians should

80. Sundberg, "Class and Ethnicity," 4.

81. Ki-Zerbo, "Historical Evolution of Education," 215–24.

82. Sundberg, "Class and Ethnicity," 5. See also World Bank Group, *Republic of Congo*, 1–4; Lumumba-Kasongo, "Congo-Brazzaville," 12–15.

be aware of the way they use ethnicity for their own interests, for "the Congolese case shows that ethnicity, in spite of the country's pronounced class conflict, can be activated at any time."[83]

To see what must be done and how, there will be a need for a committee (formed by representatives of the Congolese society as well as members of the government). My concern here is how to discover ways of reducing poverty, showing solidarity with the poor and using the wealth for the good of all the Congolese people.

Besides this, Congo-Brazzaville needs to carry out a social ethics based on its non-petroleum growth. It cannot base its economy solely on oil. There is also a need to imagine development in terms of human resources as well as in terms of a change of mentalities. The Congo experienced a Marxist-Leninist regime, and unfortunately politicians opted to change a political regime without thinking about changing mentalities. Other authors see this as a real leadership problem. In either case, an ethical solution is more than necessary.[84]

Ethical Solution in Dialogue with Some Authors

The first stage involves an ethical solution, i.e., what is the ethical solution that emerges from the ethical analysis that was made above? My answer to this question is partly inspired by the book *A Theory of Justice* by John Rawls (1971) in which the author tries to solve the problem of distributive justice or social justice. On the one hand, commutative justice is focused on individuals (equality of opportunity in the exchange). Commutative justice does not work for the Congo in as much as it only benefits individuals rather than all persons living in a society, as proposed by Thomas Aquinas and Maritain. There is also social justice which renders to each according to his economic productivity or according to his functions, his responsibilities, rank, or needs. This social justice

---

83. Sundberg, "Class and Ethnicity," 9.
84. Magnusson and Clark, "Understanding Democratic Survival," 564.

has the advantage of corresponding to the type of justice that the Congolese society needs. The advantage of social justice is that because society is composed of people, rather than merely isolated individuals, it puts people at the center of everything.

In his book *A Theory of Justice*, Rawls asserts the supremacy of what is right. Concretely, I approach this problem of justice as understood in a political science, that is, "a moral principle according to which we must assign to each what is owed."[85]

In the Congolese case, social justice is still lacking. Ultimately, it seems that commutative justice reigns while some individuals take pleasure and completely ignore the Congolese society. There is no equality in the exchange between Congolese from all sides. We have seen that those in power share oil revenues among themselves and forget the Congolese people.

In addition, there is no policy of social justice. Although the government has decided to publish the oil revenues, thanks to the advocacy of the "Publish What You Pay" campaign, the fact is that there is still work to be done.

There is also much political corruption and profiteering, almost as if we are dealing with mere utilitarians rather than politicians. In the first place, utilitarians are not concerned with justice. Second, utilitarians do not consider virtues. In other words, utilitarian theory does not pursue or achieve justice.

To solve the problem that threatens the Congolese society, I suggest that we consider the problem of justice in general because it rejects the utilitarian theory. By doing this, it will be possible to consider the problem of the common good and solidarity since the utilitarian theory refuses to help the poor.[86] My position is one that rejects the utilitarian theory because it is a theory that ignores the ethical problems in society.

I said at the beginning of this section that my answer was partly inspired by the theory of justice by John Rawls. The other

---

85. Grawitz, *Lexique des sciences sociales*, 248.

86. Because she thinks that the poor are poor because they do not want to work. In other words, poor are lazy people.

The Role of the Congolese Catholic Church

half of my answer is inspired by the CST principles and the statements of the Central African Bishops on oil.

I consider six principles as essential: option for the poor, promotion of peace, transparency and governance, attention to who benefits from oil revenues, the imperative to listen to the people, and law enforcement.

Option for the Poor

This option seems to me important because its goal is to fight against poverty that threatens more than 70 percent of the Congolese population. This is possible only if the Congolese politicians change their behavior and their way of doing politics.[87] Concretely, they must show that they love their neighbors. Love of neighbor inspires justice, for love is energy for justice. The unity of the Congo is possible only through the love that the Congolese have for each other. Until now, it is politics that divides the Congolese society.

That is why:

> As individuals and as a nation, therefore, we are called to make a fundamental "option for the poor." The obligation to evaluate social and economic activity from the viewpoint of the poor and the powerless arises from the radical command to love one's neighbor as one self.[88]

Promotion of Peace

In a country that has experienced war, it is important to continue promoting peace. "Peace must be built on the basis of justice in a world where the personal and social consequences of sin are

---

87. Congo's political history is full of grisly scenes. For more information see Massema, *Crimes de sang et pouvoir*, 20–50; Kouvibidila, *Histoire du multipartisme: Débuts*, 210–15; Kouvibidila, *Histoire du multipartisme: Marche*, 26–40; Baniafouna, *Bataille de Brazzaville*, 61–99.

88. U.S. Bishops, *Economic Justice for All*, 87.

Strategy of Action

evident."[89] These words express what is important in any given society: peace as a prerequisite for development.

Considering the history of the Congo, I propose that the values of peace and justice should be taught in our primary schools and even beyond. This is fundamental in the life of a multiethnic nation that can be considered as a home that the Congolese people build together.

Transparency and Governance

These two concepts go together and must shape the political life of the Congo. Congolese politicians should understand that one does not manage a nation as he/she manages a family household. In other words, transparency must be the leitmotiv in the management of the nation; for transparency and good governance go together.

Too often, men in power have confused the public treasury with money coming from their pockets.[90] This must stop. How? My answer to this question is as follows: all those wishing to participate in politics should declare their assets.[91]

In addition, the law must be clear on this point. Those who are guilty of embezzlement of public property must be reported to the courts, if we want effective laws, those who hijack public goods have two choices: either return the property or go to jail, and those who are found guilty of embezzlement should leave politics for a period of five or ten years. If they want to return to political life, they must provide evidence of conversion and restitution. I believe that the Congo people must have deserving leaders, not thugs whose only specialty is to steal and lie to the people.

---

89. McDonald, *Transparency*, 10.

90. For more information see Bayonne and Makimouna-Ngouallat, *Congo-Brazzaville*, 19–36.

91. This is written in the Congolese Constitution, but it is not followed.

The Role of the Congolese Catholic Church

Attention to Who Benefits from Oil Revenues

I also suggest that contracts between oil companies and the Congo be revised, because the secret nature of these contracts is a door open to non-transparency and corruption. What the bishops say on this subject is very striking:

> With the complicity of oil companies that have been paying out large sums to their benefit, these men have been able to ensure their security, to fund their political parties, and to maintain their friendships with certain dignitaries in Northern capitals. During this period, as all criticism was deemed subversive and dangerous, people were suffering in silence from the exploitation of their natural resources for the benefit of foreign powers... Our oil is still, in most cases, the private financial reserve of the powers that be. They use it as they choose for funding political activities of their sole party, diverting people's consciousness during elections, and for buying arms to ensure their safety... Our oil is sometimes mortgaged to pay off debts that have served the personal interests of certain fellow citizens.[92]

What the bishops say should challenge the political class.

The Imperative to Listen to the People

The imperative to listen to the people requires that the Congolese people can speak freely. Indeed, one cannot listen to people when they do not have the freedom to express their opinions. Until recently, the Congolese could not speak freely about oil. In Congo, the pastoral letter by the bishops in 1998 is the starting point of free speech on oil; but why in 1998 and not before? The answer can be explained by the gravity of the socio-political situation or by the high number of deaths.[93] This latter explanation will appear to be

---

92. McDonald, *Transparency*, 10.

93. Even if there are no exact figures, the general belief seems to exceed ten thousand deaths.

good if one believes the reaction of the bishops: "Our oil should be for the life and not the death of our people."

These words are evocative of those of Paul Heutching, who states that "the more that damned oil runs, the more the crisis has reached epidemic proportions to become a tragedy."[94]

Listening to people also implies being attentive to their expectations. Congolese politicians are still far from doing this. Why? This can be explained by the fact that their view of political matters is very limited or very poor. More than that, their understanding of power is limited as well.

In the book *The Art of Power*, Thich Nhat Hanh makes an insightful analysis of the art of power. He says for example that:

> Business can't exist without nonbusiness elements. Your co-workers are part of your work environment, but they are also people, a nonbusiness element. . . . Seeing the nonbusiness elements in business is the teaching of interbeing. Nothing can exist by itself alone. Everything depends on everything else in order to be. . . In the same way, business is made of nonbusiness elements, and you need to take care of the nonbusiness elements for your business to do well. . . It is perfectly possible to work in business in the light of the teaching in interbeing. The well-being of a manager and the well-being of her family are crucial to the well-being of the company itself. And the well-being of the company is crucial to the well-being of the employees and their families. Everything is connected to everything.[95]

These words are raw truth. They are valid in economic life as well as in politics. The word *interbeing* as used by the author can be replaced by that of interaction. One can indeed lead people and ignore them. Unfortunately, this is what happened in Congo. Because of oil, politicians have forgotten the existence of the people. Only when they started fighting for oil did they come

---

94. Foreword by Paul Heutching in Baniafouna, *Bataille de Brazzaville*, 9.

95. Nhat Hanh, *Art of Power*, 137–39; Mbembe, "On the Power of the False," 629–41.

THE ROLE OF THE CONGOLESE CATHOLIC CHURCH

to understood that the people exist. They only saw the need for people in military combat, but not in the political sphere.

What Thich Nhat Hanh says should be taken very seriously because interbeing is also important in politics.

LAW ENFORCEMENT

To enforce the law, the judiciary power must be independent of political power. In Congo as in most African countries, the judiciary power is intermingled with political power. Things should change, because if this distinction is not made clear in practice, the Congo will always have problems. In short, we need a true separation of power. This is a prerequisite for democracy.

This brings us to the next step.

How the Solution Fits in the Congolese Ethos: Determining whether a New Institution Is Necessary

The solution I propose focuses on liberating the Congolese people from poverty and promoting a sound management of natural resources. Such a solution is interesting because it invites Congolese people to reflect on their own problems. This solution enables politicians and populations to be constantly in contact. This contact can be assured by means of community radios where peoples' messages can be read in the national languages, in such a way that the authorities are always aware of people's needs. Thus, the authorities would not have to wait for elections to find out what local people need.

A new institution is not necessarily mandatory. Existing institutions such as the Catholic Church or any other institution of the civil society could serve as arbitrators and assure that social and economic justice is applied.

Indeed, my solution also offers a realistic and sincere way to help the poor share in the oil money. It is based on a social justice that considers all the Congolese people and not a few individuals; it rejects all forms of clientelism.[96]

Discern How the Solution Could Be Perceived in the Congolese Pluralistic Society: Possible Overall Payoffs

What I propose can be well perceived in Congo, which has a pluralistic society, since it focuses on the well-being of all Congolese people. Moreover, this solution would be well received because it involves most of the Congolese population, i.e., over 70 percent of the population of Congo.

In addition, what I propose will interest the Congolese in the first place and make them primarily responsible for their own natural resources. My solution encourages harmonious living among all ethnic groups and condemns any ethnic discrimination.

Such a solution that advocates social justice and the proper management of the common good is bound to have encouraging results, since the population is engaged in the management of natural resources.

Some Considerations

Some remarks must be made to define the scope of our reflection in terms of social analysis. According to Nimi Wariboko, "every genuine ethical analysis in any society is set in motion by four conditions."[97] The first condition is about an ultimate concern that serves as a *telos* of the Congolese society. In this reflection I have said that the ultimate concern is the mismanagement of oil in Congo. This mismanagement threatens the future of the Congolese society. The second condition concerns the obstacles and resistance to a proper management of common property in Congo. Indeed, corruption and embezzlement are obstacles for the good management of the common good in Congo. At the same time,

---

96. Magrin and Vliet, "Use of Oil Revenues in Africa," 104–17.
97. Wariboko, "Ethical Methodology," 6.

there is resistance to "what ought to be," that is, a proper management of the common good, since corruption and misappropriation of funds continue to destroy the Congolese economy. The third condition deals with "a desire to overcome such resistance"[98] to the "ought to be." In Congo, the Catholic Church and the civil society strive for a good management of oil for the well-being of all Congolese. The last condition is that "the ethical analyst must be willing to oppose his/her proffered solutions because no solution or institution is timeless."[99] In this reflection I offered solutions that can, hopefully, help Congo to move forward.

This last chapter focused on a strategy of action. Concretely, it relies on a social analysis as proposed by Nimi Wariboko. In this analysis, I identified the problem that threatens the Congolese society while pointing out why it is a problem. I then analyzed the problem as it arises in social sciences, theology, philosophy, or ethics and proposed a solution as a paradigm.

Then, I offered a series of key proposals to promote social and economic justice in Congo.

98. Wariboko, "Ethical Methodology," 7.
99. Wariboko, "Ethical Methodology," 7.

Conclusion
Promotion of Social and Economic Justice in the Matter of Oil

IN HOLLENBACH'S THE GLOBAL Face of Public Faith, the author offers an interesting description of the role of religion:

> The role of religion in forming cultural values has become central in reflection on the ethical dimensions of global politics. Recent trends leading to the globalization of politics and economics have raised many issues of notable ethical importance. They include economic justice of poor countries, including matters of aid, trade, and debt relief; the proliferation and possible use of weapons of mass destruction; the promotion of human rights and response to extreme forms of human rights violation.[1]

Hollenbach's words are applicable to the Congolese case for several reasons. First, when we look at what the Catholic Church has been doing in Congo, it is obvious that she is building cultural values that can shape the future of the Congolese people: solidarity towards the poor and promotion of social as well as economic justice. On this point, the approach of the Catholic Church is a long-term one.[2] Second, the advocacy of the Church raises questions of "ethical dimensions of global politics" as well as "internal politics." It is in this context that one must understand the

---

1. Hollenbach, *Global Face of Public Faith*, 232–32.
2. Secours Catholique, *Pour qui coule l'or noir?*, 17.

The Role of the Congolese Catholic Church

solidarity of European or American churches with the Church of Congo. Third, the advocacy of the Church includes social and economic justice relevant to the flourishing of Congo. In addition, this challenges the Congo to promote human rights and offer "response to extreme forms of human rights violation." Thus, the title of this reflection is *The Role of the Congolese Catholic Church*. "Promotion of economic and social justice in relation to oil" must be understood in this context. In Congo, "oil wealth has failed to generate development and has instead generated deep-seated corruption that retards growth."[3] Indeed, the Congolese situation raises several issues inherent in the poverty rate, which threatens its population.

This reflection has shown that the management of oil is not used in a transparent way because the Congolese population does not benefit from the oil revenues. Only a few people share in the oil money, namely, the politicians close to—and friends of—the presidential family or people involved in the oil management.

Because of these injustices, over 70 percent of the Congolese people live below the poverty line. The worsening of poverty is partly due to civil wars that afflicted the Congo in the nineties. In other words, oil played an important role in the civil wars. In addition, corruption and embezzlement are the other causes that explain the worsening of poverty in Congo.

Faced with this situation, the Catholic Church took a stand in favor of the Congolese poor. This advocacy on the part of the church can be read as a critique of the Congolese society. Indeed, there is a definite advantage to the Catholic Church assuming an advocacy role. Thus, it is in this context that one can understand the role of the church in promoting social and economic justice.

In this reflection, I have attempted to show that the concept of the common good is not respected as such by the Congolese politicians. This is contrary to the concept of African ethics, which gives much importance to the role of the community. Moreover, the common good must be respected in its reality as well as in its conception. Some principles are relevant to the flourishing of the

---

3. Afeikhena et al., "Addressing Oil Related Corruption," 9.

Conclusion

Congo about the common good: respect for the human person, respect for ethical norms for economic life, etc.

Finally, in this reflection I have made some proposals to promote social and economic justice for the Congo. Those proposals fit in well with the Congolese society because they take into consideration the Congolese ethos, namely, the history of the country, the political as well as the social situation. If the Congolese politicians respect the common good and help the population to benefit from oil revenues, there is hope for a better Congo. This is not enough, however, because a better and flourishing Congo is only possible if the judicial as well as the economic powers are independent of the dynamics of political power. This is a prerequisite for democracy and a requirement for Catholic Social Teaching. This said, I have concluded that in the matter of oil the Congolese Catholic Church is able to promote social and economic justice.

Bibliography

ACERAC. *La bonne gestion dans l'Eglise. Compte-rendu de l'intervention de Medicis Mundi International (MMI).* 8ème Assemblée Plénière. Bangui, RCA: ACERAC, 2008.
———. *The Church and Poverty in Central Africa: The Case of Oil.* Malabo, Equatorial Guinea: ACERAC, 2002.
———. *L'Eglise et la pauvreté en Afrique Centrale: le cas du pétrole.* Malabo, Equatorial Guinea: ACERAC, 2002.
———. *L'Eglise et la pauvreté en Afrique Centrale: Plaidoyer.* Bangui, RCA: ACERAC, 2008.
Afeikhena, Jerome, et al. "Addressing Oil Related Corruption in Africa: Is the Push for Transparency Enough?" *Review of Human Factor Studies Special Edition* 11.1 (2005) 7–32.
Agamben, Giorgio. *Etat d'exception. Homo Sacer II, 1.* Paris: Seuil, 2003.
———. *Means without End: Notes on Politics.* Minneapolis: University of Minnesota Press, 2000.
———. *Sovereignty and Life.* Stanford, CA: Stanford University Press, 2007.
Agenzia Fides. "AFRIQUE/ANGOLA—'Nous sommes préoccupés par les conséquences environnementales et sociales de l'exploitation des ressources du pays' affirment les évêques de l'Angola au terme de leur Assemblée Plénière." 23 mars 2006. http://fides.org/fr/news/6110-AFRIQUE_ANGOLA_Nous_sommes_preoccupes_par_les_consequences_environnementales_et_sociales_de_l_exploitation_des_ressouurces_du_pays_affirment_les_eveques_de_l_Angola_au_terme_de_leur_Assemblee_Pleniere.
———. "Delegation of African Bishops and Experts to Visit Europe to Push for Millennium Development Goals." Sep. 10, 2010. http://www.fides.org/en/news/27386-AFRICA_African_bishops_delegation_in_Europe_to_discuss_Millenium_Development_Goals.
Aristotle. *The Nicomachean Ethics.* New York: Penguin, 2004.
Badiou, Alain. *Metapolitics.* London: Verso, 2005.

Bibliography

Balogun, John. "Diversity Factors in State Construction Efforts in Africa: An Analysis of Challenges, Responses, and Options." *African Journal of Public Administration and Management* 13.1–2 (2001) 65–99.

Baniafouna, Calixte. *La bataille de Brazzaville (5 juin–15 octobre 1997)*. Congo Démocratie 3. Paris: NM7, 1999.

Banque Mondiale. "République du Congo—Vue d'ensemble." Dernière mise à jour, 8 avr. 2024. https://www.banquemondiale.org/fr/country/congo/overview.

Bayart, J.-F. "Les Églises chrétiennes et la politique du ventre: le partage du gâteau ecclésial." *Politique Africaine* 35 (1989) 3–26.

Bayonne, Omega, and J.-C. Makimouna-Ngoualat. *Congo-Brazzaville: diagnostic et stratégies pour la création de valeur. Pourquoi les crises politiques, économiques et sociales? Comment en sortir?* Paris: L'Harmattan, 1999.

Bazenguissa-Ganga, Rémy. *Les voies du politique au Congo. Essai de sociologie historique*. Paris: Karthala, 1997.

Benedict XVI. *L'engagement de l'Afrique: Africae Munus: exhortation apostolique sur l'Afrique*. Paris: Éditions du Cerf, 2011.

Berger, Peter L., and Thomas Luckmann. *The Social Construction of Reality: A Treatise in the Sociology of Knowledge*. New York: Anchor, 1967.

Bevans, Stephen, and Roger Schroeder. "Justice, Peace and the Integrity of Creation as Prophetic Dialogue." In *Constants in Context: A Theology of Mission for Today*, 348–95. Maryknoll: Orbis, 2004.

Billets d'Afrique. "Ingérences épiscopales." 106 (Sep. 2002) 5. https://francegenocidetutsi.org/BdA2002-9.pdf.

Biyela, Fred. O. "Trajectoires de l'Église de Zéphirin. Séquences d'un enchevêtrement politico-religieux au Congo-Brazzaville." *Afrique contemporaine* 267-68.3–4 (2018) 47–65.

Bratton, Michael, and Nicolas van de Walle. *Democratic Experiments in Africa: Regime Transitions in Comparative Perspective*. Cambridge: Cambridge University Press, 2002.

Brooks, Peter. "Into Africa: China's Grab for Influence and Oil." *Heritage Lectures* 1006 (2007) 1–5.

Brueggemann, Walter. *Journey to the Common Good*. Louisville: Westminster John Knox, 2010.

Bujo, Bénézet. *African Christian Morality: At the Age of Inculturation*. Nairobi: Paulines Publications Africa.

———. *The Ethical Dimension of Community: The African Model and the Dialogue between North and South*. Nairobi: Paulines Publications Africa, 1998.

———. *Foundations of an African Ethic: Beyond the Universal Claims of Western Morality*. New York: Crossroad, 2001.

Calcagno, Antonio. *Badiou and Derrida: Politics, Events and Their Time*. New York: Continuum, 1998.

Bibliography

Calvez, Jean-Yves. *Faith and Justice: The Social Dimension of Evangelization.* Saint Louis: The Institute of Jesuit Sources, 1991.

Chabal, Patrick. "The Quest for Good Government and Development in Africa: Is NEPAD the Answer?" *International Affairs* 78.3 (2002) 447–62.

Chabal, Patrick, and Jean-Pascal Daloz. *Africa Works: Disorder as Political Instrument.* Oxford: The International African Institute, 1999.

Clark, John F. "Resource Revenues and Political Development in Sub-Saharan Africa Congo Republic in Comparative Perspective." *Africa Spectrum* 37.1 (2002) 25–41.

Conférence Épiscopale du Congo. "Accueil." http://www.cecongo.net.

Conseil Pontifical Justice et Paix. *Compendium de la doctrine sociale de l'Eglise.* Vatican website, 2006. https://www.vatican.va/roman_curia/pontifical_councils/justpeace/documents/rc_pc_justpeace_doc_20060526_compendio-dott-soc_fr.html.

Copinschi, Philippe. "Governance in African-Oil Producing Countries: State, Multinational Companies and Civil Society Organizations." *CENA Internacional* 9.1 (2007) 123–39.

Curran, Charles E. *The Catholic Moral Tradition Today: A Synthesis.* Washington, DC: Georgetown University Press, 1999.

Daly, Erin, and Jeremy Sarkin. *Reconciliation in Divided Societies: Finding Common Ground.* Philadelphia: University of Pennsylvania Press, 2007.

de Beer, Hanlie, and Richard Cornwell. "Congo-Brazzaville—The Deep End of the Pool." *Africa Early Warning Programme, Institute for Security Studies* Occasional Paper 41 (Sep. 1999) 1–7.

Djereke, Jean-Claude. "Mgr Albert Ndongmo, un prophète en avance sur son temps." *Seneplus,* Sep. 4, 2022. https://www.seneplus.com/opinions/mgr-albert-ndongmo-un-prophete-en-avance-sur-son-temps.

Dongala, Emmanuel. *Johnny Chien Méchant.* Paris: Le Serpent à Plumes, 2002.

Dorier-Apprill, Élisabeth. "Les échelles du pluralisme religieux en Afrique subsaharienne." *L'information géographique* 4 (2006) 46–65.

Dorier-Apprill, Élisabeth, and Robert Ziavoula. "La diffusion de la culture évangélique en Afrique central: Théologie, éthique, et réseau." *HERODOTE* 119 (2005) 129–56.

Droits de l'Homme. "Actualités juridique pour mieux comprendre nos droits." http://www.droitsdelhomme-france.org/IMG/Constitution_de_la_Republique_du_Congo_du_20_janvier_2002.pdf.

Dulin, Antoine, and Jean Merckaert. *Bien mal acquis. A qui profite le crime?* Paris: CCFD, 2009.

Eaton, David. "Diagnosing the Crisis in the Republic of Congo." *Africa: The Journal of the International African Institute* 76.1 (2006) 44–69.

Eboussi-Boulaga, Fabien. *A Contretemps. L'enjeu de Dieu en Afrique.* Paris: Karthala, 1991.

Editions L'Harmattan. "Petrole et Violences au Congo-Brazzaville— Conférence." YouTube video, Apr. 3, 2014. https://www.youtube.com/watch?v=dF8IOlhASsM.

Bibliography

Elenga, Yvon Christian. "The Congolese Church: Ecclesial Community within the Political Community." In *The Catholic Church and the Nation-State*, edited by Christopher Manuel et al., 245–57. Washington, DC: Georgetown University Press, 2005.

Ellis, Stephen, and Ter Haar Gerrie. *Worlds of Power: Religious Thought and Political Practice in Africa*. New York: Oxford University Press, 2004.

Les Évêques du Congo. "Le Pétrole et la mission de l'Église au Congo." Conférence Épiscopale du Congo, Juin 10, 2002. http://www.cecongo.net/spip.php?article402.

Favennec, Jean-Pierre, and Philippe Copinschi. "Les Nouveaux Enjeux Pétroliers en Afrique." *Politique Africaine* 89 (mars 2003) 127–48.

Fonds Monétaire International. *Études économiques et financières. Perspectives économiques internationales. Afrique subsaharienne. Surmonter la tourmente*. Washington, DC: Fonds Monétaire International, 2009.

Freire, Paulo. *Pedagogy of the Oppressed*. New York: Continuum, 1993.

Friboulet, Jean-Jacques. "Le bien commun selon Jacques Maritain." Colloque Interdisciplinaire à la mémoire du Prof. Roger Berthouzoz O.P. (7–8 juin 2006) 1–7.

Fuellenbach, John. "The Church in the Context of the Kingdom of God." In *The Convergence of Theology: A Festschrift Honoring Gerald O'Collins, S.J.*, edited by Daniel Kendall and Stephen Davis, 221–37. Mahwah, NJ: Paulist, 2001.

Gary, Ian, and Terry Lynn Karl. *Bottom of the Barrel: Africa's Oil Boom and the Poor*. Washington, DC: Catholic Relief Services, 2003.

Gauze, Rene. *The Politics of Congo-Brazzaville*. Stanford, CA: Stanford University Press, 1973.

Gavric, Anto, and Grzegorz W. Sienkiewicz, eds. *État et bien commun. Perspectives historiques et enjeux éthico-politiques*. Colloque en hommage à Roger Berthouzoz. Berne: Peter Lang, 2008.

Giroux, Jennifer. "Africa's Growing Strategic Relevance." *CSS Analyses in Security Policy* 3.38 (Jul. 2008) 1–3.

Goldwyn, David L. "Africa's Petroleum Industry." Nov. 15, 2005. https://apps.dtic.mil/sti/tr/pdf/ADA441207.pdf.

Grawitz, Madeleine. *Lexique des sciences sociales*. Paris: Dalloz, 2000.

Haynes, Jeff. "Transnational Religious Actors and International Politics." *Third World Quarterly* 22.2 (2001) 143–58.

Hollenbach, David. *The Common Good and Christian Ethics*. Cambridge: Cambridge University Press, 2002.

———. "The Common Good in a Divided Society." *Santa Clara Lectures* 5.3 (Apr. 18, 1999).

———. "The Common Good Revisited." *Theological Studies* 50 (1989) 70–94.

———. *The Global Face of Public Faith: Politics, Human Rights, and Christian Ethics*. Washington, DC: Georgetown University Press, 2003.

———. *Justice, Peace and Human Rights: American Catholic Social Ethics in a Pluralistic Context*. New York: Crossroad, 1988.

Bibliography

Hurst, Cindy. "China's Oil Rush in Africa." Institute for Analysis of Global Security, July 2006. http://www.iags.org/chinainafrica.pdf.
Ikechukwu Odozor, Paulinus. "An African Moral Theology of Inculturation: Methodological Considerations." *Theological Studies* 69 (2008) 583–607.
Institut National de la Statistique. *Résultats préliminaires du 5e recensement général de la population et de l'habitation. Rapport.* INS: Brazzaville, 2023.
International Monetary Fund. "IMF and World Bank Announce Debt Relief to the Republic of Congo." Press release, Jan. 28, 2010. https://www.imf.org/en/News/Articles/2015/09/14/01/49/pr1020.
John XXIII. *Mater et Magistra.* Encyclical letter. Vatican website, May 15, 1961.
John Paul II. *Ecclesia in Africa.* Vatican website, 1995. https://www.vatican.va/content/john-paul-ii/en/apost_exhortations/documents/hf_jp-ii_exh_14091995_ecclesia-in-africa.html.
Kasomo, Daniel. "An Examination of Co-Existence of Religion and Politics." *International Journal of Sociology and Anthropology* 1.7 (Nov. 2009) 124–31.
Khalfan, Ashfaq, et al. "Advancing the Odious Debt Doctrine." CISDL Working Paper. 2003. https://dette-developpement.org/IMG/pdf/odious_debt_7288.pdf.
Kibangou, Hermann-Habib. "'Diagnostic' de la société congolaise: pas de progrès, sans changement de mentalités." *La Semaine Africaine* 2932–33 (29 sep. and 2 oct. 2009) 7.
———. *The Mvengian Vision of Anthropological Pauperization: A Path for Philosophical Reflection on Ntù?* Eugene, OR: Wipf & Stock, 2022.
King, Martin Luther, Jr. *La force d'aimer.* Paris: Casterman, 1964.
King, Martin Luther, Jr. *Strength to Love.* Philadelphia: Fortress, 1981.
Ki-Zerbo, Joseph. "The Historical Evolution of Education in French Speaking Africa and the Question of Development." *Utafiti* 1.2 (1976) 215–24.
Klare, Michael T., and Daniel Volman. "Africa's Oil and American National Security." *Current History* 103.673 (May 2004) 226–31.
Klein, Keith. *Elections in Congo: The Winding Road to Democracy.* Washington: International Foundations for Electoral System, 1992.
Knight, Cassie. *Brazzaville Charms: Magic and Rebellion in the Republic of Congo.* Singapore: Frances Lincoln, 2007.
Koula, Yitzhak. *Pétrole et violences au Congo-Brazzaville. Les suites de l'affaire ELF.* Paris: L'Harmattan, 2000.
Kouvibidila, Gaston-Joseph. *Histoire du multipartisme au Congo-Brazzaville. Les débuts d'une crise attendue (1992–1993).* Paris: L'Harmattan, 2000.
———. *Histoire du multipartisme au Congo-Brazzaville. La marche à rebours (1940–1991).* Paris: L'Harmattan, 2000.
Kouvouama, Abel. "Conférence nationale et modernité religieuse au Congo." *CURAPP, Questions sensibles, PUF* (1998) 388–412.
———. "Truth in Politics, and the Political Sphere in Congo (Brazzaville)." *Quest: An African Journal of Philosophy* 26.1–2 (2002) 186–96.

Bibliography

Linden, Ian. "A Global Church in the Twenty-First Century." In *Global Catholicism: Diversity and Change Since Vatican II*, 261–82. New York: Columbia University Press, 2009.

Lumumba-Kasongo, Tukumbi. "Congo-Brazzaville: Multipartyism or Illiberal Democracy." *News from the Nordic Africa Institute* 3 (2005) 12–15.

Magrin, Géraud, and Geert van Vliet. "The Use of Oil Revenues in Africa." *Ifri* (2009) 103–17.

Magnusson, B. A., and J. F. Clark. "Understanding Democratic Survival and Democratic Failure in Africa: Insights from Divergent Democratic Experiments in Benin and Congo (Brazzaville)." *Comparative Studies in Society and History* 47.3 (July 2005) 552–82.

Makouta-Mboukou, Jean-Pierre. *La destruction de Brazzaville ou la démocratie guillotinée*. Paris: L'Harmattan, 1999.

Maritain, Jacques. *Man and the State*. Chicago: The University of Chicago Press, 1951.

———. *The Person and the Common Good*. Notre Dame: University of Notre Dame, 1966.

Massaro, Thomas. *Living Justice: Catholic Social Teaching in Action*. Franklin, WI: Sheed and Ward, 2000.

Massema, Albert Roger. *Crimes de sang et pouvoir au Congo-Brazzaville. Les assassinats de Lazare Matsokota, Joseph Pouabou, Anselme Massoueme, Ange Diawara, Marien Ngouabi et Pierre Anga*. Paris: L'Harmattan, 2005.

Massengo, Gualbert-Brice. *L'économie pétrolière du Congo. Les effets pervers de la monoressource économique dans les pays en développement*. Paris: L'Harmattan, 2004.

Mbembe, Achille. "On the Power of the False." *Public Culture* 14.3 (2002) 629–41.

Mbow Mampoua, Amphas. *Political Transformations of the Congo*. Chicago: The University of Chicago Press, 2000.

McDonald, Geraldine. *Transparency: A Christian Concern: Catholic Social Teaching and the Case for Transparent and Accountable Practices in Extractive Industries*. A position paper of CIDSE, Pax Christi International and Caritas Europa, Sep. 2003.

McDonald, Geraldine, and Ian Gary. "Integrated Approaches to Peacebuilding in Africa's Petrostates." *Trócaire Development Review* 4 (2003) 87–103.

Miller, Vincent J. "Where Is the Church? Globalization and Catholicity." *Theological Studies* 69 (2008) 412–32.

Ming Wong, Kam. "Catholicity and Globality." *Theology Today* 66 (2010) 459–75.

Moumouni, Charles, et al. "Vers une gouvernance globale de la transparence extractive en Afrique". In *La transparence des industries extractives en Afrique*, by Charles Moumouni and Christophe Krolik. Québec: Presses de l'Université du Québec, 2021.

Mveng, Engelbert. *L'Afrique dans l'Église: paroles d'un croyant*. Paris: L'Harmattan, 1985.

Bibliography

———. "Impoverishment and Liberation: A Theological Approach for Africa and the Third World." In *Paths of African Theology*, edited by Rosino Gibellini, 154–68. Maryknoll, NY: Orbis, 1994.

Ndikumana, Léonce, and James K. Boyce. *La dette odieuse de l'Afrique: comment l'endettement et la fuite des capitaux ont saigné un continent.* Dakar: Éd. Amalion, 2013.

Ngoïe-Ngalla, Dominique. "La démission des hommes de prière et de culture." *Christus* 163 (1994) 366–74.

Ngouari, Appolinaire A. "Économie informelle et pratiques populaires au Congo-Brazzaville : État des lieux et perspectives." Série Comparaisons internationales, 2005. https://depot.erudit.org//id/001831dd.

Ngouma, Séraphin. "Responsibility of the Church." *New Routes: A Journal of Peace Research and Action*, Special Issue 2: "Congo Searching Peace." 7.1 (2002) 12–15.

Nhat Hanh, Thich. *The Art of Power.* New York: HarperOne, 2008.

Nyamiti, Charles. "Contemporary African Christologies: Assessment and Practical Suggestions." In *Paths of African Theology*, edited by Rosino Gibellini, 63–77. Maryknoll, NY: Orbis, 1994.

O'Neill, William, R. "African Moral Theology." *Theological Studies* 62 (2001) 122–39.

Obenga, Théophile. *L'Histoire sanglante du Congo-Brazzaville (1959–1997). Diagnostic d'une mentalité politique africaine.* Paris: Présence Africaine, 1998.

Okowa, W. J. *Oil, Systemic Corruption, Abdulistic Capitalism and Nigerian Development Policy: A Political Economy.* Port Harcourt, Nigeria: Paragraphics, 1997.

———. *The Political Economy of Development Planning in Nigeria.* Port Harcourt, Nigeria: Paragraphics, 1991.

Pedde, Nicola. "The Myth of African Oil and Gas." *CeMiSS Quarterly* 4.4 (Winter 2008) 57–60.

Pigeaud, Fanny. "Les Congolais veulent leur part de pétrole." *Alternatives Économiques*, juillet 1, 2003. https://www.alternatives-economiques.fr/congolais-veulent-part-petrole/00069166.

Population Today. "Population d'Afrique (2024)." https://populationtoday.com/fr/continents/africa/.

Portella Mbuyu, L. "Insiste à temps et à contre-temps." In *Congo-Brazzaville: Le pétrole ne coule pas pour les pauvres*, 4. Paris: Secours Catholique, 2011.

Poucouta, Paulin. *L'Eglise dans la tourmente. La mission dans l'Apocalypse.* Les éditions L'Epiphanie: Limete-Kinshasa, 1996.

Rahner, Karl. "The Function of the Church as a Critic of Society." In *Theological Investigations* 12, edited by W. D. Bourke, 229–49. New York: Seabury, 1974.

Rawls, John. *The Law of Peoples.* London: Cambridge University Press, 2001.

République du Congo. *Constitution du 20 janvier 2002.* https://mjp.univ-perp.fr/constit/cg2002.htm#pr.

Bibliography

Rickne, Johanna. "Oil Prices and Real Exchange Rate Volatility in Oil-Exporting Economies: The Role of Governance." Research Institute of Industrial Economics, IFN Working Paper 810, 2009.

Sacks, Jonathan. *The Home We Build Together: Recreating Society.* London: Continuum, 2007.

Schreiter, Robert. "Globalization and Reconciliation: Challenges to Mission." In *Mission in the Third Millenium*, 121–43. Maryknoll, NY: Orbis, 2001.

Schroeder, Roger. "The What of Mission." In *What Is the Mission of the Church: A Guide for Catholics*, 112–26. Maryknoll, NY: Orbis, 2008.

Secours Catholique. *Congo-Brazzaville: Le pétrole ne coule pas pour les pauvres.* Paris: Secours Catholique, 2011.

———. *Pour qui coule l'or noir?* Paris: Secours Catholique, 2003.

Smith, Benjamin. "Oil Wealth and Regime Survival in the Developing World, 1960–1999." *American Journal of Political Science* 48.2 (Apr. 2004) 232–46.

Sobrino, Jon. *Christ the Liberator.* Maryknoll, NY: Orbis, 2001.

———. *Jesus the Liberator.* Maryknoll, NY: Orbis, 1994.

———. "Monseñor Romero, a Salvadoran and a Christian." *Spiritus* 1 (2001) 143–55.

Sundberg, Anne. "Class and Ethnicity in the Struggle for Power—The Failure of Democratization in the Congo-Brazzaville." *Africa Development* 24.1–2 (1999) 1–29.

Sundberg, Carl. "Christianity in Dialogue with African History and Culture." *Swedish Missiological Themes* 92.3 (2004) 330–48.

Thornton, Lawrence. *Imagining Argentina.* New York: Bantam, 1988.

Tonda, Joseph. "La guerre dans le 'camp Nord' au Congo-Brazzaville: ethnicité et ethos de la consommation/consumation." *Les deux Congos dans la guerre: Politique Africaine* 72 (1998) 50–67.

U.S. Bishops. *A Call to Solidarity with Africa.* Washington, DC: National Conference of Catholic Bishops-United States Catholic Conference, 2001.

———. *Economic Justice for All: Pastoral Letter on Catholic Social Teaching and the U.S. Economy.* Washington, DC: National Conference of Catholic Bishops-United States Catholic Conference, 1998.

US Department of State. "Republic of Congo 2022 International Religious Freedom Report." https://www.state.gov/wp-content/uploads/2023/05/441219-CONGO-REP-2022-INTERNATIONAL-RELIGIOUS-FREEDOM-REPORT.pdf.

Valadier, Paul. *Des repères pour agir. Les morales sont érodées. Serions-nous sans repères pour agir? Quand la Foi nous provoque au discernement.* Paris: Croire Aujourd'hui, 1977.

Volman, Daniel. "Oil, Arms and Violence in Africa." African Security Research Project, Feb. 2003, 1–5.

Wariboko, Nimi. "Ethical Methodology: Between Public Theology and Public Policy." *Journal of Religion and Business Ethics* 1.1 (2009) 1–16.

Warner, Michael, and Kyle Alexander. "Enhancing Economic Performance in the Extractive Industries Sector: Does the Sustained Global Demand for

Bibliography

Oil, Gas and Minerals Mean That Africa Can Now Fund Its Own MDG Financing Gap?" Overseas Development Institute, Briefing Note 6. http://cdn-odi-production.s3.amazonaws.com/media/documents/844.pdf.

World Bank. *Republic of Congo: Emergency Recovery and Community Support.* Initial Project Information Document, 2003. https://documents1.worldbank.org/curated/en/153691468770720164/text/multiopage.txt.

———. *Transitional Support Strategy for the Republic of Congo.* Nov. 13, 2000. https://documents.worldbank.org/en/publication/documents-reports/documentdetail/852561468744031512/congo-transitional-support-strategy.

World Synod of Catholic Bishops. *Justice in the World.* 1971. https://www.doctrine-sociale-catholique.fr/les-textes-officiels/206-justitia-in-mundo.

Wykes, Sarah. *Avenirs Énergétiques. Les Investissements d'ENI dans les sables bitumeux et les palmiers à huile dans le Bassin du Congo.* Heinrich Böll Foundation, 2009.

Zartman, I. William, and Katharina R. Vogeli. "Prevention Gained and Prevention Lost: Collapse, Competition, and Coup in Congo." In *Opportunities Missed, Opportunities Seized: Preventive Diplomacy in the Post-Cold War Word*, edited by Bruce W. Jentleson, 265–92. Lanham, MD: Rowman and Littlefield, 2007.

Index

Abagna-Mossa, 17
Acerac, xxi, xxii, xxii, xxiii, 15, 27, 39, 40
Afeikhena, 17, 87, 104
African anthropology, 60
African black theology, 76
African christologies, 75, 78
African liberation theology, 76
African theology, 48
African (traditional) ethic, 45, 47, 50, 51
Agamben, 88, 89, 90
Agip, 6
Agenzia Fides, 27, 69
Alexander, 86
Angola, 1, 2, 8, 77
Anthropological pauperization, 67, 70, 72
Aquinas, 45, 46, 52, 58, 59, 60, 63, 64, 65, 66, 94
Argentina, 23
Aristotle, 46
Arrupe, 33, 34
Augouard, 14

Badiou, 64
Balogun, 92
Baniafouna, 96, 99

Bantu, 51
Bantu Socialism, 4
Bayart, 38
Bayonne, 97
Bazenguissa-Ganga, 4
Believers, 16, 33, 34, 35, 37, 41
Benedict XVI, xvii
Berger, 42
Bevans, 32, 33
Biayenda, 8, 36
Biblical anthropology, xv
Biblical prophet, xv, xvi
Billets d'Afrique, 77
Biyela, 9
Bishops, 25, 26, 27, 28, 33, 38, 39, 48, 76
Body, 16, 23, 58
Bouenza, 55
Boyce, 73
Bratton, 50
Brazzaville, xxvi, 1, 2, 3, 5, 9, 14, 25, 55, 77
Brooks, xxi
Brueggeman, 57
Bujo, 45, 46, 47, 48, 50, 51, 60, 63, 66, 68, 75

Calvez, 32, 34, 64

Index

Cameroon, 1, 68
Caritas Congo, 15, 16
Carrie, 14
Catholic church, xix, xxvi, xxvii, xxviii, xxix, xxx, 9, 10, 11, 12, 13, 14, 20, 22, 29, 31, 36, 41, 42, 84, 93, 100, 102, 103
Catholic Relief Services (CRS), 15
Catholic Social Teaching (CST), xx, 67, 85, 86, 88, 96, 105
CEMIR, 16
Central Africa, xxx, 1, 10
Central African Republic, 1, 3
Chabal, 49, 50, 61, 62
Chad, 3, 8, 77
China, xxi
Chirac, 8
Church / churches, 10, 11, 12, 13, 16, 21, 22, 23, 24, 26, 27, 28, 29, 30, 32, 35, 37, 38, 41, 43, 44, 68, 92, 104
Christianity, xix, 32
Christians, 9, 22, 27, 32, 36, 38, 41, 78
Christology, 75, 76, 78
CIDSE, 15
Civil society, xxviii, 29, 43, 84, 92, 100, 102
Civil war, 7, 10, 35, 38, 69, 79
Clark, 81, 94
Clientelism, 101
Common good, xxii, xxviii, 45, 48, 52, 53, 54, 56, 57, 58, 59, 63, 64, 65, 66, 87, 89, 91, 92, 93, 101, 102, 104, 105
Community, xxix, 46, 47, 48, 51, 58, 59, 63, 64, 65, 66, 100, 104
Commutative justice, 60, 65
Compendium of the Social Doctrine of the Church, 29
Conférence épiscopale du Congo, 16
Congo Basin, xxx, 3, 10
Congo-Brazzaville, xx, xxi, xxii, xxiii, xxiv, xxvii, xxviii, 1, 3, 4, 5, 7, 12, 15, 46, 54, 56, 59, 82, 92, 94
Congo-Oubangui, 55
Congolese episcopal conference, 15, 16, 30
Congolese bishops, 33, 49, 69
Congolese economy, 6, 7, 10
Congolese Episcopal Conference, 15, 16
Congolese People, xxv, xxviii, xxix, xxx, 10, 33, 35, 36, 38, 42, 48, 49, 50, 54, 61, 62, 68, 75, 78, 81, 84, 85, 88, 89, 91, 92, 94, 95, 98, 100, 101, 103, 104
Congolese politics, 7
Congolese society, xxvii, xxix, xxx, 12, 13, 16, 17, 20, 25, 30, 31, 34, 35, 36, 37, 41, 43, 53, 64, 68, 69, 70, 80, 81, 84, 85, 91, 92, 94, 95, 96, 101, 102, 104, 105
Conseil Pontifical Justice et Paix, 30
Copinschi, xix
Corinthians, 32
Cornwell, xxvi, 82
Corruption, xx, xxv, xxvi, xxix, 40, 41, 43, 57, 68, 72, 76, 80, 98, 101, 102, 104
Critic of society, 24, 25, 27, 30, 31
Critique, xxx, 13, 20, 24, 25, 31, 104
CSC (Congolese Trade Union), 5
Curran, 64
Cuvette, 55
Cuvette-Ouest, 55
Czuba, 36

Daly, 36, 37
Daloz, 49, 50
Death, 98
De Beer, xxvi, 82
De Brazza, 3
Democracy, xix, 10, 61, 100, 105
Democratization, 13, 69

Index

Democratic Republic of Congo / Congo Kinshasa, xvi, 1, 2, 9
Departments, 55
Development, 58, 97
Diamonds, 7
Dignity, 62, 64, 65, 66, 76
Distributive justice, xv, 65
Divine empathy, xv
Djereke, 27
Djoué-Léfini, 55
Dolisie, 14
Dongala, 67, 78, 79
Dorier-Apprill, 9
Dulin, 71

Eaton, xxvi, 80
Eboué, 3
Eboussi-Boulaga, xix, 11
Economic and social justice, 45, 46, 48, 51, 60, 62, 67, 105
Education, 57, 93
Elenga, 11, 12, 13, 15, 38, 41
Elf, 10
Embezzlement, xx, xxv, xxvi, xxix, 40, 68, 69, 72, 76, 80, 97, 101, 104
Episcopal Conference of the Congo, 11, 13
ENI, 6
Ethics, xxvii, 47, 49, 58, 80, 102
Ethical analysis, xxvii
Ethical discourse, 46, 59
Ethnicity, 81, 83, 93, 94
Ethnic groups, 35, 54, 55, 93
Ethos, 25, 44, 67, 76, 81, 85, 90, 91, 105
Evangelization, 11, 13, 29, 31, 32, 43
Évêques du Congo, 26, 49
Exodus, xv
Ezekiel, xv

Favennec, xix
France, 3, 5, 8, 10
Freire, 70

French Equatorial Africa, 3
Friboulet, 57, 58
Fuellenbach, 41
Function of the Church, 43

Gabon, 1, 3
Galatians, 32
Gamboma, 14
Gandhi, 33
Gary, xxi, 20, 69
Gas, 10
Gassongo, 36
Gauze, 82
Gavric, 46
Genesis, xv
Giroux, 86
God, 33, 39, 48, 59, 60, 65, 88, 90, 91
God of justice, 33, 65
Gold, xxviii, 30
Goldwyn, xx
Governance, 78
Grawitch, 33, 46, 60, 95

Halbecq, 36
Hanh, 99, 100
Haynes, 13
Henriot, 86
Heutching, 99
Hollenbach, 12, 57, 59, 64, 65, 103
Holy Ghost Missionaries, 14
Home, 55
Human dignity, 48, 49
Human person, 45, 48, 61, 62, 66, 105
Human rights, xix, xxvi, 43, 64, 104
Humanization and exploitation and management of oil revenues, xvii,
Hurst, xxi
Hydroelectricity, xxviii

Ignatius Loyola, xxix, xxx
Ikechukwu, 75
Impfondo, 14

Index

Inculturation, 75
Injustice, xxix, 32, 33,
Institut national de statistiques, 2, 77
International monetary fund, 73
Iron, xxviii

Jeremiah, xv
Jesus, xvi, xvii, 26, 36, 78
Jesus Christ, 37, 39
John XXIII, 22, 62, 86, 87
John Paul II, 31, 86
Judiciary power, 100
Justice, 21, 32, 39, 43, 57, 58, 60, 64, 96
Justice and peace, xix, 16, 17, 20, 44, 51

Karl, 20, 21
Kasomo, 12
Kema, 17
Khalfan, 74
Kibangou, xv, xvi, xix, 68, 92
Kikongo, 83, 93
Kimbaguist (Church), 9, 37, 76
Kimbangu, 9
King Iloy (King Makoko), 3
King (Jeff), 74
King (Martin Luther), 33
Kings, xv
Kinkala, 14
Kinshasa, 9, 41
Ki-Zerbo, 93
Klare, xxi
Klein, 1, 4
Knight, 3, 4, 6, 7, 71
Kolelas, 79, 81
Kombo, 5, 9
Kongo kingdom, 2
Kouilou, 55
Koula, 6, 8, 70
Kouvibidila, 5, 96
Kouvouama, 5

La Semaine Africaine, 9

Law enforcement, 100
Leca, 46
Le Floch-Prigent, 70
Lékoumou, 55
Liberalism, 57
Likouala, 55
Linden, 20,
Lingala, 84, 93
Lissouba, 5, 7, 79, 81, 82, 83
Loango, 14
Love of neighbor, 33, 34, 96
Luckmann, 42
Luke, 78
Lumumba-Kasongo, 80, 93

Management of the common good, xxvii, xxviii, 46, 47, 50, 51, 54, 57, 58, 101, 102
Management of oil, xxiv, 21, 50, 51, 60, 71, 86, 87, 102, 104
Management of natural resources, xix, xxv, 19, 28, 92, 100
Manamika, 17, 18, 19
Manganese, 6, 10
Magnesium, xxviii
Magnusson, 94
Magrin, 101
Makimouna-Ngouallat, 97
Makouta-Mboukou, 82
Makosso, 19, 40
Maritain, 34, 45, 46, 52, 56, 57, 58, 59, 60, 63, 66, 94
Marxist-Leninist regime, 5, 94
Massengo, 6
Matthew, xvi, 85, 86,
Massamba-Débat, 3, 4, 8
Massaro, 88, 89
Massema, 96
McDonald, xx, xxi, xxii, 15, 21, 41, 69, 86, 87, 91, 97, 98
Meckaert, 71
Mbembe, 99
Mbochi, 81, 82, 84
Mbow, 4, 5, 7

Index

Merckaert, 71
Miller, 12
Milandou, 77
Militia, 7, 79
Ming Wong, 12
Mismanagement, xxvi, xxix, 35, 41, 69, 70, 75, 76, 81, 101
Mitterand, 5
Mizonzo, 17, 18
Money, 49, 54, 84
Monsengwo, 41
Mouanga, 17, 19
Moumouni, xx
Mounzeo, 19, 40
Muslim (s), 9, 36, 37
Mveng, 67, 68, 69, 70, 71, 72, 73, 74, 76, 78

National Conference, 9, 36, 37
Natural gas, xxviii
Natural resources, xxix, 10, 21, 42, 53, 72
Ndikumana, 73
Ndongmo, 26
Negro-African thought, 48, 68
Neo-patrimonialism, 61
Ngoïe-Ngalla, 11, 22, 27, 28
Niari, 55
Nigeria, 77
Ngassongo, 17, 18, 19
NGO, 21, 87, 92
Ngoma-Foumanet, 17, 18
Ngouabi, 3, 4, 8
Ngouari, xxiv
Ngouma, 38, 43, 84
Nkayi, 14
Nkeni-Alima, 55
Nkossa, 83
Nhat, 99
Non-believers, 16, 33, 34, 35, 37, 38, 41
Nyamiti, 67, 75, 76
Nzika, 18, 19

O'Neill, 47
Obenga, 1, 82
Oil, xix, xx, xxi, xxii, xxiii, xxiv, xxv, xxvi, xxvii, xxviii, 6, 7, 8, 10, 26, 33, 42, 46, 48, 49, 50, 51, 57, 67, 69, 71, 73, 76, 77, 84, 85, 90, 98, 99, 104
Oil boom, 7, 71, 87
Oil companies, 70, 71, 98
Oil and war, xxii
Oil and economy, xxii
Oil and the human and the ecology, xxiii
Oil and ethnicity, xxiii
Oil money, 50, 100
Oil, natural resources, xxiii
Oil and politics, xxi
Oil and suffering, xxiv
Oil revenues, xxv, 8, 33, 48, 49, 69, 70, 72, 75, 76, 87, 77, 95, 104, 105
Okowa, 77
Opangault, 82
Ontology, 68
Option for the poor, 84, 88, 96
Orthodox, 76
Ouesso, 14
Owando, 14

Palaver, 48, 50
Parable, 55
Psalms, xvii
Paradigm, 67, 91, 92
Paul VI, xvi, 22
Pauperization, 69, 70, 72, 73
Pax Christi, 15
Peace and Justice Commission, xxi, xxix, 17, 19
Pedde, xxi
Philosophy, 67, 80, 102
Phosphate, xxviii
Pigeaud, 26
Plateaux, 55
Population Today, 77

Index

Pointe-Noire, xxi, 2, 14, 55, 83
Political leaders, xxviii, 6, 10, 25, 36
Political realm, 16
Political violence, 4, 10
Politics, xxv
Portella, 15, 24, 30, 31, 69, 87
Possible overall payoffs, 101
Potash, xxviii
Pool, 55
Poor, 32, 33, 36, 44, 70, 73, 76, 84, 90, 95, 103
Poucouta, xvii, 11, 22, 27, 28, 29
Poverty, xx, xxi, xxv, xxx, 30, 32, 41, 43, 50, 61, 69, 70, 71, 72, 74, 75, 76, 77, 81, 89, 90, 94, 100, 104
Poverty line, xxv, 9, 49, 52, 61, 70, 87, 104
Principle of solidarity, 20, 89
Promotion of Social and Economic Justice, xxix, xxx, 53, 65, 67, 88, 100, 102, 103, 104, 105
Prophetic empathy, xv
Protestant (s), 9, 36, 37, 76
Proverb (s), 50
Psalms, xvii
Public realm, xxvi, 31
Public sphere, 15
Publiez ce que vous payez/Publish What You Pay, 17, 19, 20, 40, 87, 92, 95

Rahner, 12, 21, 22, 23, 24, 25, 30, 31, 37, 43
Rawls, 94, 95
Religion, 41, 103
Republic of (the) Congo, xxii, xxv, xxvii, 1, 2, 3, 10, 20, 14, 50, 53, 61, 71, 77, 78
Responsibility /responsibilities, 16, 24, 25, 37, 41, 43, 50, 51, 60, 84
Rickne, xx

Role, xix, 10, 16, 38, 40, 41, 43, 47, 50, 88, 103, 104
Romans, 32
Roman Catholic Church, 12, 14, 21, 29, 40
Romero, 33

Sacks, 45, 46, 52, 54, 55, 56, 60, 66
Saint Paul, 32
Saint Peter, 40
Sangha, 55
Sarkin, 36, 37
Sauvaire, 79
Schreiter, 37
Schroeder, 20, 32, 33
Sassou-Nguesso, 4, 7, 79, 82, 83
Second Vatican Council, 64
Secourscatholique, xx, xxi, xxvi, xxvii, 15, 20, 21, 33, 50, 103
Sienkiewicz, 46
Significance of community, 93
Smith, xxi
Sobrino, 33, 78
Social analysis, 30, 67, 92, 101, 102
Social (ethical) analysis, xxv, 21
Social ethics, xxvii, 45, 54
Social and economic justice, xix, xxvii, xxviii, 20, 45, 46, 47, 52, 53, 60, 61, 62, 66, 68, 100, 102, 104
Social critique, 21
Social justice, xxvii, 33, 44, 60, 61, 95, 100
Society, 54, 55, 58
Soldiers, 7
Solidarity, 39, 44, 50, 89, 91, 103, 104
South Africa, 76
Spirituality and ethics of empathy, xv, xvi,
Strategy, 67
Strategy of action, 67
Subsidiarity, 88, 89
Sudan, 77
Sundberg, 2, 80, 93, 94

Index

Theological discourse, xxvii
Theological level, 24
Theology, 67, 76, 78, 102
Thomas (B), 74
Thornton, 23
TotalFinaElf/Total Energies, xxi, 6, 7, 8, 10, 70
Totalitarianism, 58
Transparency, xix, 19, 21, 42
Timber, 7, 10
Tonda, 50, 80, 81, 82, 83, 84

Uranium, xxviii
USA, 8
US (catholic) bishops / American bishops, 15, 20, 46, 60, 61, 62, 63, 64, 66, 96, 104

Van de Walle, 50
Valadier, 90
Values, 54, 103
Victims, 79

Violence, 28, 29, 75, 91, 93
Virtues, 35, 54, 57
Vliet, 101
Vogeli, xxvi, 80
Volman, xxi, xxiv, 8, 10, 77

War, xx, 76, 77, 79, 80, 81, 82, 84, 87
Wariboko, xxv, xxvii, xxviii, xxix, 67, 85, 87, 101, 102
Warner, 86
Wealth, 49
Western thought, 68
Womb, xv
World bank, xxiv, xxv, xxvi, 69, 93
World synod of catholic bishops, 34
Wykes, 2

Yhombi-Opango, 4
Youlou, 2, 3, 4, 9, 82
Zartman, xxvi, 80
Ziavoula, 9
Zinc, xxviii, 10

www.ingramcontent.com/pod-product-compliance
Lightning Source LLC
Chambersburg PA
CBHW051943160426
43198CB00013B/2274